❧ I'll Get Back to You ❧

Other Books by Robert L. Shook

Robert L. Shook is a best-selling author who has written more than 40 books. Three of his books on selling are:

The Greatest Sales Stories Ever Told:
From the World's Best Salespeople

Hardball Selling: How to Turn the Pressure On
Without Turning Your Customer Off

Successful Telephone Selling in the '90s
(coauthored with Martin D. Shafiroff)

I'll Get Back to You

156 Ways to Get People to Return Your Phone Calls

Robert L. Shook

Eric Yaverbaum

McGraw-Hill

New York   San Francisco   Washington, D.C.   Auckland   Bogotá
Caracas   Lisbon   London   Madrid   Mexico City   Milan
Montreal   New Delhi   San Juan   Singapore
Sydney   Tokyo   Toronto

Library of Congress Cataloging-in-Publication Data

I'll get back to you : 156 ways to get people to return your phone
  calls and other helpful sales tips / [compiled by] Robert L. Shook,
  Eric Yaverbaum
     p. cm.
    ISBN 0-07-057721-8 (pbk.)
    1. Telephone selling. I. Shook, Robert L.
  II. Yaverbaum, Eric.
  HF5438.3.I55 1996
  658.8´4—dc20   96-20583
                                                  CIP

McGraw-Hill

A Division of The **McGraw·Hill** *Companies*

1 2 3 4 5 6 7 8 9 0 DOC/DOC 9 0 1 0 9 8 7 6

ISBN 0-07-057721-8

*The editor for this book was Susan Barry, the editing supervisor was Fred Dahl,
and the production supervisor was Pamela Pelton. It was set in New Caledonia by
Inkwell Publishing Services.*

Printed and bound by R.R. Donnelley & Sons Company

This publication is designed to provide accurate and authoritative information in
regard to the subject matter covered. It is sold with the understanding that the
publisher is not engaged in rendering legal, accounting, or other professional
service. If legal advice or other expert assistance is required, the services of a
competent professional person should be sought.

> *From a declaration of principles jointly adopted by a committee
> of the American Bar Association and a committee of publishers.*

 This book is printed on recycled, acid-free paper containing a
minimum of 50% recycled, de-inked fiber.

McGraw-Hill books are available at special quantity discounts to use as
premiums and sales promotions, or for use in corporate training programs. For
more information, please write to the Director of Special Sales, McGraw-Hill, 11
West 19th Street, New York, NY 10011. Or contact your local bookstore.

To my beautiful mother, Belle Shook.

Bob

To my parents, Harry and Gayle Yaverbaum.
You make your son proud.

Eric

❧ Contents ❧

Section 6
Great Voicemail Messages   89

❧ Acknowledgments ❧

First and foremost, Eric thanks his brilliant partner, Jon Sawyer, whom he credits for much of the success Jericho Promotions has enjoyed during the past 11 years.

Eric also thanks his wife and best friend Suri Nisker, who gives him her full support and who, in particular, never complained about his long hours at the office working on this project. "Everyone should be lucky enough to have a best friend like mine," Eric says.

Bob is quick to add that he too is fortunate to have a best friend: his wife, Elinor, who is equally supportive of his writing career. "El is always there for me," he states, "except when I need someone to fix my lunch."

Eric acknowledges Becque Olson, whom he refers to as his "incredible assistant." "Becque was always there to make sure this book happened while I was running my public relations firm. Her attention to detail and focus on doing a thorough job made this an enjoyable process."

As usual, Bob acknowledges his assistant, Maggie Abel, who he thinks is also incredible. Maggie did everything from transcribing interviews, to editing copy, to making sure everything was properly organized. "It's easy to write a book," Bob says, "when somebody as able as Maggie Abel does all that work!"

Eric is deeply appreciative of his agency's key people, whom he considers it an honor to work with on a daily basis. These wonderful individuals are: Sherri Candel, Greg Mowery, Beverly Stowe, Roger Bilheimer, Hope Freundlich, Neil Goldberg, Marci Greenberg, Toni Herron, Liat Jehassi, Hope Kaufer, Laurie

Kratz, John Krisiukenas, Reggie Lewis, Felicitas Lozada, lan Madover, Kim Morgan, Tammy Palmer, Sabrina Porter, Marcia Potash, Tim Schramm, Anna Suslovsky, and Helen Tarleton.

And, of course, Bob and Eric give special acknowledgment to Tia Dobi, who did the lion's share of the research on this book. Not only did Tia interview most of the people whose stories appear in this book, her charm and persuasive powers got them to return her calls!

The two authors also acknowledge Susan Barry, McGraw-Hill's exceptional executive editor who worked with them from start to finish on this book. "Actually," they both point out, "this book was Susan's brainstorm. She conceived the idea to write a book on how to get people to return phone calls." And, as Bob reveals, "In the beginning I was reluctant to write it. However, Susan eventually convinced me *I had to do it.* I said I would, but only if I could collaborate with somebody with the hottest, most creative public relations firm in town. This is where Eric and his partner Jon came into the picture. They tossed a coin to see who would collaborate with me. They never did explain who won the toss!"

We also acknowledge Phil Ruppel, publisher at McGraw-Hill. In our book, he's one of the best people in the publishing industry—a real gentleman and a pleasure to work with. A special thanks to our agent, Al Zuckerman, president of Writers House, who did his usual fine work.

Last but not least, we thank the wonderful participants who shared their stories and ideas on how they get people to return their phone calls. Without their willingness to share, this book could not have been written.

ROBERT L. SHOOK

ERIC YAVERBAUM

❧ Introduction ❧

Everyone has experienced the frustration of not having a telephone call returned. Perhaps the only people who don't have this problem are VIPs, such as U.S. Senators, CEOs of large corporations, and superstars like Barbra Streisand and Robert Redford. Of course, they weren't luminaries all their lives. So even they have at some time had a receiver slammed in their ears.

Generally speaking, busy and important people are the more difficult to get through to, second only to people who owe you money! So it's not only the rich and famous who are unavailable when you "reach out and touch someone."

Some of the VIPs in this book relate methods they used to get their calls returned in their earlier days when they were just ordinary folks. Others share why, currently, they return one call but not another.

This book reveals 156 wonderful tips on how to get people to return your calls. All have been field-tested—and *work!* While we personally espouse a few tips, most are methods devised and proven by some of the most interesting people in America. In researching this book, we contacted hundreds of super salespeople, business leaders, and VIPs ranging from entertainers to professional athletes. Because we interviewed a wide array of people from different parts of the country, you have a large selection of techniques to choose from. There is something for everyone, making it easy to pick the right one for you!

Most interestingly, our research also revealed that, for millions of Americans, making phone calls is an essential part of their typical work day. Their success directly hinges on the percentage of returned calls they receive. In spite of this obviously important determinant of their performance, most continue to apply the same tired telephone techniques they've used for years—no matter how poor the results! It's a sad fact that many businesspeople and salespeople are hypnotized by routine, unaware that just a little time and effort spent brushing up on telephone skills triggers dramatic payoffs!

We believe that properly applying the techniques shared in this book will vastly increase the number of your returned calls. Better yet, the relatively small cost and effort are temporary, while your gains are permanent.

One thing we discovered early in our research was that certain people fare much better than others in getting calls returned. We were intrigued to learn that the success ratios had little to do with the obvious, such as a great telephone voice, fancy title, etc. Instead, it had everything to do with technique. Yet not all our interviewees could explain why their success ratio was so high. Those who had instinctively developed an effective technique often had not thought it out; it just "evolved." But this book offers you a distinct advantage: *Your* success won't be left to chance!

The tips in this book run the gamut. Some no-nonsense techniques get right to the point. Others employ a bit of subterfuge, while a few are out-and-out gimmicks. The reason several work so wonderfully is their shock value! As you'll discover, some methods require a little investment, but 99 percent are free! From the whimsical to the outrageous, the tips in this book are intended to amuse. After all, it sometimes takes a good sense of humor to keep things in perspective, particularly if you've been on hold for 15 minutes, or after you've made 30-something calls and still haven't gotten one call-back!

Often, you'll discover that a witty or humorous approach is just the ticket to getting your call returned. So no matter how serious the nature of your call, a touch of humor may break the ice with a resistant person. As an extra bonus, you'll discover that humor serves as a superb stress reliever—at both ends of the receiver! For the record, you don't want to come across as "stressed out." If you do, people can sense this in your voice.

When you use some of these ingenious and intriguing tactics, you communicate a lot about yourself. You may show that you have a sense of humor, that you don't take yourself too seriously, and that you bring tension-relieving wit to the table. And by your determination to make the connection, you show that you are the bearer of an important message. A subliminal message—that you are witty, industrious, and resourceful—projects the image of a person they want to talk to!

Whatever works to get your call returned is fair game. Everything! For instance, you'll discover fabulous ways you never dreamed of to use your fax machine, and never again will you be at a loss for words when that formerly dreaded voicemail asks you to leave your name and number. There are even suggestions about sending, via overnight courier or messenger, "surprise packages" to unsuspecting prospects.

Keep in mind that some of the approaches in this book have to be tailor-made to fit your personality. It's not only what you say but the way you say it. For instance, suppose you leave a message with a secretary or on voicemail that says, "Call me—it's about the state lottery," or "Call immediately—I'm with the IRS." When your call is returned and the truth is learned, the response can vary from anger to laughter. Most often, it depends on your winning personality. You might greet the person with a friendly admission, such as "All right, you didn't actually win the lottery, but I sure got your attention, didn't I?" Or, "Really now, aren't you relieved I'm not with the IRS?" With a charming technique, you stand a good chance of being well received, despite your deception.

As you can see, a lot of your success depends not on the other party's mood, but on *your* mood. This means you have to like people so much that your friendliness comes across on the telephone. Conversely, if you're resentful or have a chip on your shoulder, this too is picked up. With this in mind, we advise you to get yourself psyched up before you place your call. Your mood is reflected in your voice!

Remember, too, if only one idea in this book works for you, you have received your money's worth many times over. However, we recommend choosing a few favorites to test. You'll find that some can be implemented immediately, while others may take a little rehearsal. Keep in mind that, when it comes to getting calls returned, nobody bats a thousand, and one method may not work with everyone. If one method doesn't get the result you seek, don't worry—just try a different one. And, if something you particularly believe in doesn't get quick results, don't give up. Keep on dialing! When you find one that's a winner for you, practice it, refine it, and play it to the hilt!

Section One

❦ No Nonsense, No Bull: ❧ Straightforward Approaches

In this first section, we'll start with a round of conservative techniques to appease our readers who want to go strictly "by the book." These are solid approaches, the kind you'd expect a professional sales manager working for a blue chip company to employ.

Admittedly, these are mild in comparison to some of the bolder methods described elsewhere in the book. In short, what you read in this section doesn't involve the risk of the more enterprising, aggressive techniques.

This section offers effective ways to get people to return your calls. Unlike some other methods in this book, these won't make waves or involve confrontation. If you favor a conservative approach, you'll find what you are looking for in this section and won't have to read any further.

❧ Your Boss Will Appreciate It ❧

Buck Rodgers

This former vice-president of marketing at IBM is known as a legendary figure at the giant computer company. As you will see, Buck's direct approach gets right down to business.

"My name is Buck Rodgers with IBM. I'd like to speak to Mr. Miller," I'd say to the gatekeeper. The IBM name would get me some attention, but it was still up to me to get my foot in the door.

If I encountered resistance, I'd say, "Look, I know you haven't met me, and I know your boss is a busy person. I also know that I have something really worthwhile to give him that will help him run his business, and he would want you to provide me with an opportunity to talk to him."

Sometimes the gatekeeper would reply, "I'm sorry but he's busy right now. May I have your number, and I'll have him call you."

In this situation, I said, "I know, from having my own secretary, what your job entails. I know it's tough for you to decide whom he speaks to. I also recognize that he's busy, but believe me, what I have to say will be well worth his time. And I know he will appreciate that you gave me a chance to speak to him."

❧ Wearing the Stockholder's Hat ❧

John McGill

President of Tele-Communications, Inc., in Brook Park, Ohio.

When I called George, the CFO of Oxymoron Controls, a local manufacturer of slow-speed instant replay equipment, I knew that every day he wasn't a customer of ours, his company was losing money. The new and more effective system we could provide would cost less than the maintenance costs for the refurbished system Oxymoron had installed ten years ago. This knowledge made it all the more frustrating when the enticing messages I left on his answering machine went unanswered.

One day I decided to place an order with my broker for a few Oxymoron shares. This enabled me to leave another message for George, describing myself as an apprehensive stockholder who wanted to speak to him.

George called the following morning. "What can I do for you, sir?" he inquired.

"I have a grave concern about the corporate philosophy on preserving shareholder value through cost reductions achieved by implementing new technology," I replied. Needless to say, this got George's full attention.

We have since installed one of our PBX systems at Oxymoron, and George is now learning to use his new voicemail so that he can better protect my vested interests!

Authors' Comment: When calling on senior managers of publicly owned corporations, this approach certainly gets their attention.

❧ A Mutual Friend ❧

Richard Connolly, Jr.

One of the nation's top stockbrokers, Richard Connolly, Jr. works out of the PaineWebber office in Boston.

Sometimes when I call a prospect at home, a family member who has been trained to screen his calls asks, "Does he know what it is in reference to?"

Obviously, this person is trying to evaluate who I am and ultimately is the decision maker on whether I will speak to my party. With this in mind, I say, "We have a mutual friend, *John Doe.*" I do this even when the mutual friend has nothing to do with the reason I am calling, which is most often the case.

If we don't have a mutual friend, and I know the prospect has an interest in golf, as I do, I say, "We share a common interest and I was calling to discuss it."

If the party is not in, I always leave a message stating my name and that I will call back. I believe it's always good to get my name in front of someone.

❧ Let's Make a Deal! ☙

Steven Finkel

*President of Professional Search Seminars, a St. Louis–based training firm that
specializes in executive search, recruiting, and employment. An author and lecturer
on four continents, he is regarded as the world's premier trainer in his field.*

As the president of several "headhunting" firms for many years, I have developed a number of effective techniques to enable me to consistently reach senior or midlevel executives on the telephone. What's critical after my initial conversation, however, is getting them to respond—promptly—when I call a *second* time!

This requires me to sell them on how they can benefit by returning my future calls. I do this by asking them to make a commitment to me. At the end of my first call I say, "Look, John, I'll make a deal with you." Having said this, I pause to wait for him to ask, "What kind of deal?"

"I won't waste your time. If you hear from me, it will be for only one of two reasons," I continue. "Either I've got the candidate to whom you need to speak, or I need more information from you to help me find that candidate. Does this seem reasonable?"

Again I pause and wait for his consent. Then I add, "However, if I do call and miss you, either of these two reasons I've mentioned requires an immediate return call from you. Does that pose a problem?"

By adding this at the *end* of the conversation, it's most likely to stick in their minds. And by saying, "I'll make a deal with you," and obtaining a commitment through several minor-point closes, I make them feel obligated to return my call. Naturally, I'll send some follow-up correspondence to them, which further solidifies that they are expected to return my future calls quickly.

By following this specific technique, I increased my "returned call percent" significantly—with an equivalent increase in production!

❧ An Offer They Can't Refuse ❧

Barry Kaye

*Recognized as the nation's top life insurance agent. An expert on estate taxes,
he is founder and chairman of Wealth Creation Centers,
a firm specializing in estate tax cost discounts.*

Before I call a prospect, I do my homework so that I know something about him or her. My clients today have extremely high net worths, and when I leave a message on their voicemail, I want to say something that gets their attention:

> Good morning, Sam, this is Barry Kaye, and I have something brand new for you. I don't want to waste either your time or mine, so if what I have to say makes sense to you, please call me. My number is 999-9999.
>
> How would you like to buy a very substantial life insurance policy and borrow the premium to pay it on a one-time basis? What's more, you'll never have to pay interest for the rest of your life, and the only time the loan and interest would be paid off is upon your death. And when it is paid off, Uncle Sam will pay off half the loan! If you have any interest, please call me—and if you don't, I will understand.

I have an incredible offer, and it's hard to imagine the type of people who qualify for this proposition not returning my call. This is why most of them do. And once they call me, I know I have a bonafide prospect!

Authors' Comment: You don't have to be a life insurance agent to capture the interest of a prospect. This approach works no matter what your product is. Of course, you must use creativity to verbalize exactly what pushes your prospect's hot button. Barry Kaye is a leader in his industry because he clearly understands the needs of his clientele.

✎ Say No More ✍

Anonymous

A prominent businessperson who wishes to remain anonymous tells us that, when the gatekeeper asks, "Who shall I say is calling?" he gets his call put through every single time.

I just say, "Tell him his sex therapist is on the phone." She's usually too embarrassed to ask me anything else!

Authors' Comment: Before you say this, we recommend that you be sure that both the gatekeeper and your prospect have a good sense of humor!

❧ A Subtle Approach ❧

Charles Williams, Jr.

Vice-president of sales for Reynolds & Reynolds in Dayton, Ohio.

If somebody doesn't return my calls, I do some investigating to find out who he reports to. With this information, I say to his gatekeeper, "It is my understanding that Mr. Smith reports to Mr. Jones. Is that correct?"

"Yes."

"What is Mr. Jones' number?"

This approach is very effective because it subtly suggests that, if Mr. Smith does not return my call, I intend to call his superior.

Authors' Comments: Be very careful when deciding whether to use this approach with a prospect, since it can occasionally backfire.

Getting the Scoop from the Competition

Hardwick Simmons

Chief executive officer of Prudential Securities in New York City.

As a young stockbroker starting my career in the securities industry, I figured out a wonderful way to get my foot in the door to talk to the senior management of major corporations. After reading the prospectus of a company that was about to go public, I'd let my fingers do the walking through the local Yellow Pages to get the names of its competitors.

When the gatekeeper answered, I'd say to the gatekeeper, "This is Wick Simmons. I'm calling to ask Mr. Smith for his advice about XYZ Company, because I am considering selling it to my clients."

My calls were almost always returned. This surprised my colleagues, because I was getting return calls from prospects who were considered extremely difficult to get through to. I learned that many top managers were quite willing to serve as my teacher. Additionally, just as I sought information from them, they were looking to me for information. I discovered they wanted the latest inside scoop on their competition. Through this approach, a high percentage of these individuals became so interested in a competing company, I'd open an account with them so that they could participate in the offering.

> **Authors' Comment:** This is an excellent approach for stockbrokers. However, it can work for anyone who owns stock in a publicly held corporation.

❧ Who I'm *Not!* ❧

Naura Hayden

Author, actress, singer, composer, producer, and editor. Her best-selling books include How to Satisfy a Woman Every Time *and* Everything You've Always Wanted to Ask About Energy But Were Too Weak to Ask!
She resides in New York City.

When leaving a message—whether by voicemail or to an assistant—for someone I've never met, I say:

> Hi, I'm Naura Hayden, and I'm *not* with the IRS, I'm *not* selling insurance, I'm *not* looking for a job, and I *don't* want to borrow any money, but I *do* want to talk to Mr. Smith. Please repeat my message to him and let him know it's important to call me. Thank you. I really appreciate it. My phone number is 999-9999.

❧ Getting Down to Business ❧

Colleen Howe

*President of Power Play International, Inc. and owner/president of Power
Play Publications, Inc. She and her husband, Hockey Hall of Famer Gordie Howe,
live in Traverse City, Michigan, where she manages the companies'
interests and other business affairs.*

I have experienced a couple of times that, during the negotiating stage of a business deal, there can be a breakdown of communication in which the other party stops returning telephone calls. This generally happens when someone has a change of heart or has not been truthful or sincere. They then avoid having to tell someone or write someone of their change of heart. Meanwhile, getting them to call you back is extremely frustrating and time-consuming.

When I see the red flags of avoidance, I take action. "Look," I tell Mr. Smith's assistant, "this is the fifth call I've made at the times Mr. Smith has suggested, and now I'd like you to put my call through to him, or I'm not going to hang up until he comes to the phone."

Assistants get very concerned when this is done. Although I am straightforward and firm, I say in a nice way:

> This will be the last phone call Mr. Smith will have to take, but I do need to talk to him now. Please tell him that I am not angry. I just want to get this resolved immediately, one way or the other, so that we can get on with our other responsibilities. I need to find out where we stand in our relationship and continuation of business. Neither of us has the time to continue repeated calls which lead only to more phoning.

After I have expressed my thoughts, I wait it out. I may be put on hold for a few minutes, but my call does get Mr. Smith on the phone.

❧ Your Biggest Nightmare ❧

C. Britt Beemer

Founder and CEO of America's Research Group, one of America's premier marketing research firms, headquartered in Charleston, South Carolina.

I have no problem getting by the gatekeeper who asks, "What is the nature of your call?"

I simply reply, "Just say I was hired by his competition to put him out of business."

After this reply, my call is always put through. When I'm asked who hired me, I say, "When you hire me to consult with your company, I'll tell you."

Authors' Comment: Any consultant, attorney, or accountant can use this technique—even a salesperson who is selling a service to a business.

～ Hi, This Is Del Calling ～

Del Reddy

*Writer and book promoter in the Detroit area, Del takes
great pride in telling the following story.*

I called Alec Mackenzie, who is the author of *The Time Trap,* the classic best-selling book on time management that has sold more than half a million copies. Mackenzie probably knows more about why people don't have enough time than anybody else in the world. Prior to calling him, I had already read Mackenzie's book. In it, he recommended placing a high value on time and never wasting it. Furthermore, he abhorred intrusion. No wonder I was a bit apprehensive as I dialed his number.

I called him at his residence, and his son answered.

"Who's calling?"

I sensed that even his children had been trained to screen his calls. "Please let him know Del's calling," I answered, striving to sound casual and upbeat.

After three to four minutes, I could faintly hear them discussing the call in the background. Finally, Mackenzie came to the phone. "Who is this?" He seemed cautious.

"Hi! This is Del, Dr. Mackenzie. I really enjoyed reading your book, and I'd like to ask you some brief questions in regard to a book I'm writing."

I started right in on the interview and met with no resistance. Afterward, he said, "You know, most strangers who call don't get through to me. But when my son told me, 'Del's on the phone,' I thought perhaps you were an old friend. Had you given your last name, I wouldn't have taken the call, but now that we've talked, I'm glad we did."

Also, he mentioned that no one else had done that when calling him, and he said he really liked that approach. Everybody else gave their first and last name. He said that he was pleased and that he enjoyed our conversation.

I felt very good after we hung up because the man who put time in its place, the father of time management, had taken the time to talk to me.

❧ Let's Talk Business! ❧

Tara Schuchmann

Managing director of Tara Capital Partners I, L.P., in Dallas, Texas.
Prior to forming her own investment company, she was one of
Merrill Lynch's top stockbrokers.

My clients are highly successful individuals who consequently place a high value on their time. Knowing this, I follow an unwritten rule with them. I call them only when I have something important to tell them. My conversations with them never involve small talk; when they pick up the phone, I get right down to business.

Over a period of time, they *know* that when Tara contacts them, they should take the call. If they're not available at the moment, I leave a message requesting them to return my call—and they almost always get back to me shortly thereafter.

❧ I Wouldn't Be Doing My Job . . . ❧

Charles de la Motte

Director of training development for Formal Systems, Inc.,
in Princeton, New Jersey.

Early in my career, as a green salesperson, I was told to call top executives early in the morning to catch them before they were too busy. I followed this advice and I was able to get through to the national executive director of sales at Ciba-Geigy. Unfortunately, I had no other strategy. Once I had him on the phone, I didn't prepare myself to go beyond that! Luckily, I was able to think quickly on my feet. Since he headed a vast sales organization, I knew he appreciated good salesmanship. With this in mind, I said, "Sir, I am certain you would feel I was negligent in my job if I failed to request an in-person interview with you. After all, a person in your position expects a knowledgeable salesperson to do this."

Then, without hesitating, I continued, "Would next Wednesday at 10:00 or next Thursday at 1:00 be good for you?"

"Put me down for Thursday at one, young man," he said with a chuckle.

❦ It's Personal ❧

Charlie Abel

Head of Charles G. Abel Agency, Inc., in Jonesboro, Arkansas, a firm that develops management and sales computer software for companies that make sales appointments by telephone. He is the former state manager of American Family Life Assurance Company (AFLAC) and past executive vice-president of National Investors Life Insurance Company (NILIC). The following technique is one he used with much success during his career with AFLAC.

I have a standard reply when the gatekeeper asks, "What's the nature of your call?"

"It's personal," I answer. Most often, this is all that's necessary, and she'll put my call through.

However, if she asks again, I repeat softly, but with emphasis, "I said it is personal."

When Mr. Decision Maker gets on the line, after I identify myself as representing AFLAC, I explain:

> Mr. Decision Maker, I told your secretary that the nature of my call is personal. Let me elaborate. We offer an employee benefit program for the care and treatment of cancer. It's a program that 60 percent of your employees would want to buy and be willing to pay for themselves. However, had I mentioned the program to your secretary, and if you were to decide not to make it available to your employees, it might have put you in a bad light, and I did not want to do that.

> Now I am sure you can appreciate why I had to be somewhat mysterious with your secretary.

✌ I'm Not at Liberty . . . ✌

Kent Clark (a fictitious name)

*Vice-president and senior financial consultant with a large
national securities firm in Chicago.*

A secretary asks, "What's this in regard to?" Even if I'm making a cold call I say, "Oh, he knows. It's a personal matter."

I feel comfortable with this for two reasons. First, the employer's investments *are* personal, and, second, I'm not kidding anyone when I make a solicitation call. An astute businessperson knows what's going on.

I also have a pat answer for the secretary who asks, "What company are you with?"

"I'm with Mr. Clark's office," I say, but I don't mention my firm by name because that would tip off the prospect that I'm selling securities. Generally, it's not necessary to say anything else. Now and then, however, an aggressive gatekeeper asks, "What do you do?"

In a polite and professional manner, I answer, "Ma'am [or sir] I want you to know I am not at liberty to share that information with you."

And if there is still resistance, I add, "This is very confidential and personal."

Now the gatekeeper may continue to resist by saying, "I can't put your call through unless you give me some information." Then, with all the empathy I can drum up, I say, "Ma'am [or sir], I *totally* respect where you are coming from. But *please* understand *my* position. I simply cannot tell you anything more than that I'm from Mr. Clark's office. *Please,* as I said, it is *important.*"

When all else fails, as soon as I hear, "I'm sorry, I can't . . ." I cut the assistant off and say, "That responsibility is yours, and it's a decision you have to make. Here's my name and number. I have to go."

I believe in taking the bull by the horns rather than allowing an assistant or secretary to decide whether I talk to the boss. This way, I am in control of my own destiny—not other people.

Section Two

❧ A Touch of Humor ❧

While the more serious-minded individual might feel a bit awkward with the contents of this section, humor has a time and a place in the business world. After all, when used appropriately, humor is a superb door opener. *A word of caution in advance, however: What's funny to one person may not be funny to another.* So you are advised to use discretion. When the other party isn't receptive to what you think is humorous, it's no laughing matter! Still, at the right time and with the right person, the marvelous tools in this section open many previously closed doors.

❧ The Award ❧

Bruce McNeilage

A successful Northwestern Mutual Life rep in Hollywood, Florida,
Bruce isn't shy about letting a secretary or assistant know how
he feels when someone repeatedly fails to return his calls.

After leaving several messages with no response, I say to the gatekeeper, "I need to know the correct spelling of Mr. McClusky's full name. I'm having a plaque engraved with his name for an award."

She carefully spells the name and then asks, "What's the award for?"

"It's the award for *The Most Unreturned Phone Calls* during the past six months."

This always gets a laugh, and a returned call.

❦ A Noble Call ❧

Amanda Uhry

*Head of a successful medical and health care public relations agency
in New York, Amanda tells us this one.*

I simply leave a message with the gatekeeper or on voicemail: "This is the Baroness von Uexkull," and I state my number.

Sometimes I use Countess of Athalone or Countess von Ardigon. Take your pick. Since everyone wants to know why he or she is getting a call from the Euro-nobility, I always get my calls returned. This technique always works—*always!* Of course, when they find out who I really am—I am not nobility—they think it's hilarious.

By the way, this works wonderfully when making reservations at chic restaurants that are booked for months in advance. As a matter of fact, it worked last night at Gramercy Tavern!

❧ VIPs and Their Cars ❧

Melissa Rivers

Show business personality Melissa Rivers leaves this brief message when she calls somebody "important." It works because it plays on people's vanity.

I say, "This is your mechanic, Hans, calling about your car," and I leave my number.

If you do this, I guarantee you will get a call back. Important people just aren't important without their important cars.

> **Authors' Comment:** They say a man's car is an extension of his alter ego. In this respect, Ms. Rivers is right on target!

❧ It May Work for ❧
Walter Cronkite, But . . .

Walter Cronkite

*News commentator Walter Cronkite suggests, facetiously, of course, that a good
way to get through to hard-to-get persons is to find out about their hobby in
advance. Then, he advises, use this ammunition when a secretary asks in an
ice-cold voice, "And what shall I tell him it is in reference to?"*

"It's about the fire at his golf club!"

Or, depending on his hobby, you might say, "It's about the accident with his
boat!"

I confess, just how one explains the subterfuge when the elusive party is on
the phone is the second test of ingenuity. Frankly, I've never dared try it.

Authors' Comment: If you're Walter Cronkite, you're likely to get away with
this one. But for everyone else, it's going to take a lot of fast talking to keep
people on the line.

The authors of this book say this is a good time to be 100 percent truthful, so you might want to say something like this: "I read in a wonderful,
newly published book called *I'll Get Back to You* that Walter Cronkite suggested this approach to get through to a VIP who's otherwise impossible to
contact on the telephone. But now that I've got you on the line, let me tell
you about. . . ."

❧ And Joan Rivers Says . . . ❧

Joan Rivers

When I leave a message, I don't say, "Let's talk!" I say, "Congratulations! You have just won the $10 million lottery. Please call Joan immediately at 999-9999."

> **Authors' Comment:** Here too, as in the case of Walter Cronkite, celebrities can get away with a lot that the rest of us cannot. Again we suggest you refer to the book and tell the other party that you're just following the advice of Joan Rivers.

❧ You're in My Will ☙

Anonymous

*A television producer at ABC's 20/20 who asked us not to use his name,
describes a technique his friend uses on him.*

I'm overworked and admittedly am bad at returning calls. When my friend couldn't get through to me, he left the following message: "Hi, Joe, it's me, Bill. I just wanted to check the spelling of your last name, because I'm making out my will."

I felt guilty and called him back immediately. In fact, Bill still pulls this one on me from time to time, and I always return the call!

❧ The IRS Is Calling ❧

Sig Munster

*Senior vice-president with Dean Witter, and one of the firm's
top-producing stockbrokers, Sig tells what he did after making
several unsuccessful calls to a potential client.*

I kept leaving my name with his secretary, but he never returned my call. Finally, out of frustration, when she asked, "Who may I say is calling?" I simply said, "Tell him an IRS agent is on the line."

She immediately put my call through and when he said he thought I used a sneaky tactic, I agreed with him. "But I finally got you on the phone, didn't I?" I replied.

We both had a good laugh. I suppose he was relieved I wasn't really an IRS agent. Then we got down to business, and he's been a good client ever since.

Authors' Comment: Be careful with this one. Some people might not find humor in your impersonation of an IRS agent.

❧ Sing a Song ❧

Sy Sperling

*Founder of the Hair Club for Men (of "I'm the president and a client" fame),
Sy believes in doing his homework before cold-calling a prospect.*

Several years ago, I found out that a potential client sang in his church choir. Knowing this, when the guy answered the telephone, I broke out in a rendition of "Old Man River, that old Man River, he just keeps rolling, he just keeps rolling. . . ." He loved it, and I was in like Flynn.

> **Authors' Comment:** When our researcher, Tia Dobi, called Sy to interview him for this book, she left her name and number on his answering machine. Tia was also charmed by a Sperling song. He left a song on her machine: "Do you want to go for a cup of Tia? Why don't you and I-ia go for a cup of Tia?" Tia loved the message, and claims that although she gets a lot of comments on her unusual name, Sy's song was the most original.

❧ A Million Bucks! ❧

Peter Golenbock

Best-selling author (Personal Fouls, Bronx Zoo) Peter Golenbock claims he always returns calls and therefore doesn't like it when other people don't.

I'm a writer who sits by himself all day, and I'm thrilled to have someone to talk to in the middle of my day. Sometimes I even answer the long surveys about luncheon meats or household detergents to have some human interaction in the heart of the afternoon.

Conversely, I hate it when people do not return my phone calls. The worst antagonist I can recall was a former TV agent of mine who, without warning one day, just stopped returning my calls. I had no idea, since I thought we were friends. After two weeks of getting no response from him, I took it personally. Finally, I threatened to fire him. Even that did not work. And when I did, in fact, fire him, he took it personally, threatening that I would never work in the TV business again, which was interesting because I had never worked in TV in the first place!

A few years later, after I wrote *Personal Fouls*, causing the firing of beloved basketball coach and TV personality Jim Valvano, another powerful TV agent told me that I had offended so many important people in TV sports that I would never work in the TV business again.

But over the years I have become more sophisticated when it comes to getting people to call me back. My toughest targets are usually former players I wish to talk to for a book I am writing.

My messages are usually left on answering machines or voicemail. First, I try gratitude. "I would really be soooo grateful for a few minutes of your time."

Pleading comes next. "Puhleeeeeeeaze call me back."

If that fails, I go into the begging mode. "If you don't call me, I'm going to be in such trouble. I *beg* of you, call me!"

Real men don't fall for any of the above, and so when that doesn't work, I resort to my most successful method: bribery. "If you talk to me, I will pay for your time."

And most of the time that works.

Once I told a former player I would pay him a million dollars if he would call me back. He called. "Where's my million bucks?" he growled. I then told him about the book I was writing, and I said to him, "If you talk to me, you'll get a million dollars worth of publicity."

He laughed at my brazenness and gave me the interview.

The Amazing Kreskin

*The world's foremost mentalist has no problem when he leaves
a message on an answering machine.*

I just say, "Stop what you are doing right now and focus. If you're in the office, set your gaze on the wall clock or something in front of you on your desk." (At night, I say, "If you're at home in bed, set your eyes on the bed post.") After a pause, I say, "Concentrate. This is the Amazing Kreskin and you *will* call me back."

That's what I use, and it works every time.

One that also works and that anyone can use is to leave a message on someone's voicemail or answering machine: "Hello, Bob! Listen, about that message that I left earlier today—disregard it. Thanks. Bye." Leave your name and number. Of course, there wasn't an earlier message, so they are dying to call you back to find out what they missed!

Authors' Comment: You don't have to be the Amazing Kreskin to use this second technique effectively!

⧽ This Is the President Calling ⧼

Shelby H. Carter, Jr.

*In 1979 through 1981, Shelby served as president of Xerox Corporation's
U.S. operations of the Information Systems Division during the
Jimmy Carter administration.*

I couldn't resist leaving messages stating, "This is President Carter calling." It worked especially well when I'd call otherwise hard-to-reach politicians, although my southern accent isn't anything to brag about!

> ***Authors' Comment:*** Shelby also mentions that, whenever he has to return a call from a person he doesn't want to talk to, he calls during the lunch hour, when the other party is probably unavailable!

❧ Fire! ❧

Michael McCafferty

After serving as an IBM rep and enjoying several successes in the computer industry, Michael founded TELEMAGIC, a firm that produced the number-one sales software in the world.

Before I got into the TeleMagic adventure, for a short while I worked for a friend's company that sold candles to Catholic churches. It was always the priest who made the buying decision, but, to my misfortune, when I called to set up an appointment to see the priest, buying candles wasn't high on his list of priorities. I suppose it's the nature of the job, but a priest is a pretty busy fellow—you know, with confessions, marriages, funerals, masses, and so on. So you can imagine the response I got when I called and asked to speak to the priest about selling him my candles.

It didn't take me long to figure out that a salesperson who wants to sell wares has to figure out a way to be on top of the customer's priority list, because if you're at the bottom, forget it! With this in mind, I came up with a great line to get me through when someone would ask, "What's it all about?"

"It's about the fire in the church!" I'd say with a sense of urgency. This really got their attention.

If somebody said, "I didn't know the church was on fire," I answered, "No, this is about the fire *in* the church, and I have to talk to Father about it."

This worked wonderfully, and my call was always put through. Fortunately, priests usually have a good sense of humor, especially when they turned out to be fellow Irishmen. After we both enjoyed a good laugh, he would set up an appointment for me to call on him.

❧ Check with the Missing ☙ Persons Bureau

Alan Abel

Author of Don't Get Mad, Get Even, *Alan is nationally known as a media hoaxer. He once had his obituary run in* The New York Times, *even though he's very much alive. Several years ago, Abel made national news when he was interviewed on television as the founder of the Society for Indecency to Naked Animals (SINA). When we called Abel, we expected a great story from him—and he didn't disappoint us.*

A while ago, after I had sent a screenplay to a movie producer in Hollywood and talked to him several times, I began to get the runaround. Once when I called, his secretary told me, "He's out of the country and won't be back for several weeks." Now I had happened to see him driving down Wilshire Boulevard that morning, so a few hours later, I called again. This time, the secretary told me, "He's out to lunch, and I expect him back by 2:00."

For the rest of the day, each time I called, he was tied up on another line.

In frustration, I called the Los Angeles Police Department and filed a missing persons report on him. The following day, two police officers showed up at the producer's office! Would you believe that he was so astounded that I had been concerned about him, that he called me back immediately. The next day, we signed the deal!

❧ It's Jack Nicholson Calling ❧

Michael King

CEO of King World Productions Inc. in Los Angeles, Michael tells a terrific story about how he once sold a syndicated television show to the general manager of WBTV in Charlotte, North Carolina.

Early in my career, I was a performer, and I must admit I was pretty good at impersonations, especially of Jack Nicholson.

Once Joe Hutchinson's secretary told me when I called, "I'm sorry but Mr. Hutchinson isn't in his office. He's at the far end of the building complex. Can I give him a message that you called?"

In my best voice, I said, "Just tell him that Jack Nicholson is waiting for him."

"Oh!" I could nearly hear her gasp. "Can he return your call, Mr. Nicholson?"

"No, I'm sorry, but I'll be out of the country for three months. But it's okay. I have something very important to discuss with him, but it will have to wait."

"No, no, Mr. Nicholson, I'll run over to the warehouse to fetch him. Would you give me a few minutes? This is a pretty big place here, you know."

She ran off to get Hutchinson, and when he got on the phone, his puffing and heavy breathing told me the secretary was right about the distance.

"Hello, Hutch. What took you so long? Jack had to leave. It's me, Michael King, how are ya?"

With that, we both had a belly laugh, and, even though he was a little upset, I sold him a show.

> ***Authors' Comment:*** It takes a lot of chutzpa to use this. You have to pick and choose when to use it, or you could fall flat on your face! It also requires that you do a convincing impersonation!

❧ It's a Dog's World ❧

Carolyn Farb

*A community leader in Houston, Texas, Carolyn is one of the nation's
most highly regarded fundraisers. She has raised millions of dollars
for civic and charitable causes.*

Recently, I served as chairperson and hosted the first-ever annual telethon for Houston's Society for Prevention of Cruelty to Animals. Considering that the majority of the area's corporations had already prepared their 1995 philanthropic budgets, our fundraising mission was quite a challenge. The only thing we had going for us was that most people can related to the protection and care of animals.

One of my calls was to former First Lady Barbara Bush, whom I had previously met. After I described the telethon to her assistant, I said, "Please tell Mrs. Bush that my reason for calling is to see if First Dog Millie might phone in a pledge during the telethon to Bogie—my dog, who is serving as the telethon's official mascot."

Not long afterward, an excited volunteer on the phone bank received a personal call from Mrs. Bush registering Millie's pledge. The former First Lady's participation gave an exciting sparkle to our campaign.

❧ The Skeleton ❧

Terrie Williams

New York City–based Terrie Williams heads a public relations firm bearing her name. The author of The Personal Touch, *she represents some of the nation's top-ranked entertainers and corporations.*

Every now and then, I'll find I have placed several calls to a reporter who hasn't called back. When this happens, I sometimes send him or her a little rubber skeleton—you know, the kind you see on Halloween that dangles on a string—in a small coffinlike box. Along with the package, I send a note: "This is me, waiting for you to call me back." It's amazing how many people respond to this!

❧ The Call No Secretary ❧ Dares to Question

Sydney Biddle Barrows

Sydney tells her method, which can work only for her.

Getting people to take or return my call is one of the few problems *I don't have.* I make sure to give the receptionist or secretary my full name, and, if I'm not sure the boss will contact me, I add, "You might know me better by my nickname, the Mayflower Madam."

This gets everyone's attention. And since everyone is curious about why I might be calling, I always get my call returned.

Authors' Comment: The authors admit that the Mayflower Madam has a hook that works well for her but not necessarily for anybody else. We like this one because it illustrates the influence a celebrity-type person can have— even when she has some notoriety.

Section Three

❧ Persistence ❧

Perseverance is an attribute necessary for getting people to return your phone calls. When you call VIPs who work on tight schedules, you should anticipate having to place more than a single call. As you read some of the anecdotal material in this section, you'll observe the virtue of hanging in there even though your calls are not immediately returned. Most importantly, stay enthusiastic about your mission. Keep positive thoughts when you encounter rejection. Negative feelings only compound your phoning problems. You must be thick-skinned. Leave the negative experience of a previous phone call behind you and move on!

Remind yourself that successful people admire persistence. They can identify with it because, most likely, this is what helped them get to the top. So don't despair—persevere.

❧ Persistence ❧

Georgette Mosbacher

In 1988, Georgette purchased La Prairie, a business she sold two years later when she started Georgette Mosbacher Enterprises, a New York–based company offering a modestly priced line of beauty and skin care products. She is married to Robert Mosbacher, former Secretary of Commerce during the Bush Administration and currently Chairman of the Houston–based Mosbacher Energy Company. Georgette uses a simple alternating approach.

I phone. I fax. I phone. I fax. I phone. I fax. I'm sure they call me back just to get rid of me, but eventually, I talk to them.

Authors' Comment: It pays to be persistent.

❧ Congratulations, Jerry Seinfeld ❧

Steven Ekstract

In charge of advertising in the Eastern United States for The Hollywood Reporter.

Not long ago, our magazine published a special issue to salute the 100th episode of *Seinfeld.* Being a big Jerry Seinfeld fan myself, I anticipated selling a lot of ads. In particular, I could hardly wait to pitch it to American Express. After all, with Seinfeld as their spokesperson, it seemed a natural.

When I contacted American Express, however, I was told I'd have to talk to the company's ad agency, Ogilvy & Mather. That's not what I wanted to hear. As a veteran in the business, I know that ad agencies have multilayers of media people and account people, as well as other layers of executives whose jobs seem to exist for the sole purpose of saying no to anything even remotely related to advertising that wasn't planned at least a year in advance! Several calls that I placed to the agency confirmed that this was not the route to take. I heard every excuse in the book, from "There is no budget to run the ad" to "I never heard of *The Hollywood Reporter.*"

After making no headway with Ogilvy & Mather, I started calling American Express again. When I called the advertising director, I got a "no" right off the bat. Then I tried his boss, the vice-president of marketing. After 15 calls, faxes, and messengered letters, I still hadn't gotten past square one. Time was running out. With only one day to go before the issue closed out, I decided to go right to the top and call the president of American Express. Through a friend of mine who worked at the company, I got the president's office phone number.

Before placing the call, I did my homework. I found out the president was working hard to make major changes and improvements. I also read articles about Jerry Seinfeld's concern about who he represented; he had carefully scrutinized American Express before consenting to be its company spokesperson. Suddenly a light bulb lit up over my head!

I wasn't able to speak directly to the president, but I did get the ear of his assistant:

> Would you please tell him that a tremendous opportunity exists for American Express to take out a full-page congratulatory ad in *The Hollywood Reporter*, which is the leading publication in the entertainment industry. This is an opportunity to tell Seinfeld how the company feels about him, and all of his peers will witness it. From what I hear about your boss, I think this is an opportunity he won't want to pass up.

"Would you put everything in a letter and fax it to my attention?" she asked. "I'll make sure he sees it."

Shortly afterward, my fax went out, and that same morning the president called me to say it was a go. "Somebody from the ad agency will call you before noon, West Coast time," he assured me. Sure enough, with the minutes before the deadline ticking away, I received a call to book a full-page, four-color ad that the agency put together especially for the issue.

I learned an invaluable lesson: When you believe in something and know it's right, don't allow the mediocrity that often exists within the ranks of midlevel management stop you. Go to the top! The people at the top are there because they are able to take action when good opportunities present themselves.

❧ A Lesson in Perseverance ❧

Rich Luisi

*Prior to being named a vice-president for the Electrolux Company,
based in Marietta, Georgia, Rich was its number one salesperson—
an impressive achievement in a sales organization of 15,000 representatives.
The following account—by our researcher—explains what happened when
Luisi was contacted to participate in this book.*

Since Rich Luisi and Bob Shook were personal friends, my initial call to Luisi was easy. I called Luisi's personal number and got right through to him. When I asked him for material for this book, he replied simply, "Never give up. Be persistent. Be tenacious!"

"Uh—that's it?" I asked.

"That's it."

"I agree," I said, "but we could really use a longer story with a little more substance."

"A longer story? A little more substance? Mmm, let me sleep on that one. Call me back next week," he said in a friendly voice.

"Any particular time?"

"How about 2:15 on Monday afternoon?" he volunteered.

That Monday, I called and Rich said, "You're certainly punctual, but you caught me at a bad time. Would it be okay if we rescheduled this interview for Friday at 9 A.M.?"

"No problem," I said.

When Friday morning came, I called him at nine on the dot, but his assistant said, "Mr. Luisi regrets being unable to talk to you today. He said to tell you he's been thinking about you and he would like to pencil in a telephone interview for this Monday at 5:45."

I now had a long weekend to ponder what to do if the interview fell through a third time. Well, the third time's a charm, I said to myself. The more I thought about it, the more determined I became to do the interview. And I remembered Bob telling me: "Rich is my good friend, and, of all people, I know he'll have a good story for you."

On Monday afternoon at 5:40 sharp, I dialed Luisi's personal number. By this time he recognized my voice. "Would you mind calling me back in 15 minutes?" he asked. What could I say? So I consented, knowing full well I risked losing him.

At exactly 5:55 P.M., I called back, only to reach his answering machine!

I wasn't about to give up. I called Electrolux's main number, and when a computerized operator's voice came on, I punched in L-U-I-S. Bingo! "Hello, Rich Luisi speaking."

I introduced myself, and he said, "I'll be right back with you." Once more I was put on hold. This time, it didn't matter how long I had to hold, I wasn't about to hang up.

After what seemed like an eternity, Luisi came back on the line. "Mr. Luisi," I said in a firm voice. "You promised me a story—"

"You don't need a story," he interrupted. "You lived it. You've demonstrated to me what I told you when we first talked: 'Never give up. Be persistent. Be tenacious!'"

It took a few seconds for his message to sink in. "Thank you very, very much, Mr. Luisi," I said.

"By the way," he said congenially, "do you own an Electrolux?"

Authors' Comment: When we heard this story, it was in the form of a complaint. When we explained that it was a great lesson and we'd use it in the book, our assistant saw it in a different light. Understandably, it embarrassed her, and she requested that we not use her name in this story.

❧ It's Your 800 Number! ❧

W. H. "Butch" Oxendine

President of Oxendine Publishing, a publisher of student magazines, Butch sells a magazine called Student Leader *to colleges and universities across the country.*

After making 36 calls to a small, privately owned school in Ohio without making any headway, hearing neither a "yes" nor a "no," I sent a fax that I hoped would get the admissions director's attention.

The school has a toll-free number for high school seniors and transfer students to use when calling the admissions office. To keep my long distance telephone calling expenses down, I use such 800 numbers to make my sales calls. I'm very persistent. Until I have told my story and determined that I can't help prospects, I keep hanging in there, because I believe I can help them.

In my fax, I stated:

> Sir, upon reviewing my records, I've discovered that in the past three years, I have mailed you two letters with updates about our services, sent you three faxes, and placed 36 calls to you. Am I mistaken that we can't be of service? I've been calling on your 800 number, and I don't want to be a nuisance if I can't help you. So won't you please take a few minutes and give me a call when it's convenient?

This usually gets a response, which saves me time and effort, even if it's a "no." When I mention that I'm using his 800 number, my prospect realizes that *it's costing him money not to return my calls*!

Authors' Comment: While this works on some occasions, you risk running into a few people who will tell you in no uncertain terms that they do not appreciate your tying up their 800 numbers.

❧ 35 Calls Later . . . ❧

Peter Kash

Venture capitalist, Senior Manager Director of Paramount Capital
and Castle Group. Traveling to more than 20 countries, Peter has successfully
coraised over $150 million in private and public financing for biopharmaceutical
companies. He has hosted Financial News Network's "International Spotlight" and
has served as adjunct associate professor of Marketing at PolyTechnic University.
Not long ago, after making 35 calls to the office of Sherrill Neff, senior
vice-president of corporate development of U.S. Health Care,
the nation's largest HMO, Peter Kash had built what he considered a
friendly relationship with his prospect's secretary.

She's a lovely woman, always cordial and receptive, but I never got through to Neff.

Since I was not making any progress, this time I said, "This is my 35th call, and I'd really like to speak to Mr. Neff. Please tell him that I'll call back on Thursday at 9:00 A.M."

"Certainly, Mr. Kash."

"Be sure to mark it on his calendar, so he'll be expecting my call," I said politely, ending our brief conversation.

When I called back, she informed me that Neff was busy. "I'll hold," I replied, which I did for 10 minutes. Finally, Neff picked up the receiver.

"Mr. Kash, I am very busy . . ."

"Mr. Neff," I interrupted, "I'm going to speak to you for 30 seconds, and if you don't like what I have to say, I won't bother you anymore." Then I talked about Neose Technologies, Ltd., a company I thought U.S. Health Care should invest in.

As a result of that 30-second telephone conversation, I was able to set up a two-hour meeting a couple of weeks later. Another month passed and we had a second long meeting, and, a month after that, U.S. Health Care invested $2 million in Neose.

Neff couldn't be happier. He became so intrigued with Neose, he became its president. Since then, the company has raised an additional $30 million in private and public financings.

Authors' Comment: In our book, anyone who puts in 35 calls before he gets through is a winner. And, boy, did Kash's persistence pay off!

❧ The Early Bird ❧

Bettye Hardeman

For several years during the 1980s, Atlanta's Bettye Hardeman was the number-one residential real estate salesperson in the nation. Here's her secret.

Whenever I had difficulty getting through to VIPs at their offices, I'd call them bright and early at their homes. It always worked wonders. Why? I suppose, since few people ever call them early, they're not used to it. Or it may be that I simply caught them off guard. Then, too, successful people are generally early risers; so they respect other people who also start to work early.

> **Authors' Comment:** Before you call people in the early hours of the morning, we suggest that you determine beforehand whether they are indeed early risers. Waking someone out of a deep sleep who is not a "morning person" is a poor idea.

❦ What Am I to Think? ❧

Dorothy Leeds

A professional speaker, Dorothy Leeds is the noted author of Power Speak *and* Smart Questions. *She lives in New York City.*

I do a lot of business with Fortune 500 companies. After I've had some contact with a prospect but I don't hear back from the party, I leave the following message on the answering machine in an upbeat, conversational tone:

> I know you are very busy and you wouldn't have asked me to send those materials if you weren't interested. Imagine how frustrating it is from my end, to keep trying to reach someone who promised to call me back and doesn't do it. So I'll just assume that you really think what I have is not right for you and you're not interested. I'm sorry about this, and here's my number because I hope that I'm wrong and you'll call me.

My tone is warm and friendly, and when I leave this message, more than 65 percent of the time, my call is returned.

❧ A Seed of Doubt ❧

Stan Witkowski

Director of Strategic Client Initiatives at Prudential Securities in New York City.

After I make several calls to Mr. Big, if he doesn't get back to me, I'll call his secretary. "This is Stan Witkowski. Is Mr. Big there?" I say. Before I get an answer, I ask in a low voice, "Is he still with the company?"

This rarely fails to get me a return call. Sometimes Mr. Big says, "Of course I'm still with the company. Why would you intimate anything else to my secretary?"

In a polite manner, I answer, "Well, since I didn't hear back from you, I wasn't sure you were still there."

Once in a while, if Mr. Big is somewhat insecure, he may say, "Why do you ask? What have you heard?"

While some people may think this approach is offensive, I think it's offensive when somebody doesn't return a phone call!

Authors' Comment: As Stan Witkowski says, this approach may offend certain people. We suggest you use discretion.

❧ A Thin Line ❧

Robert Shook

*After making several calls without getting past the gatekeeper,
from time to time author Robert Shook uses this approach:*

"Helen"—by this time, I am calling her by her first name—"I've called many times, and I have yet to talk to Mr. Jones. I realize that there's a thin line between persistence and making a pest of myself. I hope I'm not making a pest of myself. . . ."

Then I pause. She usually says something like, "Not at all, Mr. Shook. You're simply being persistent."

"I wouldn't be calling so much if it wasn't important. I'd certainly appreciate it if you'd put my call through."

"Let me see what I can do," she's likely to reply.

Authors' Comment: It's amazing how effective this line is. It works well because it catches people off guard, putting them in an awkward position and making them feel obligated to agree—and to help.

Section Four

❧ Great Faxes ❧

Without question, the fax machine has become America's number-one selling tool since the telephone. It's quicker than using a messenger service or overnight delivery—and a lot less expensive.

Of course, since just about every business today owns a fax machine, sending a facsimile is nothing new. A lot of the fax sales techniques that originally opened the door for salespeople have since become old hat. In this section, however, we worked extra hard to find the most clever and ingenious techniques to pass on to you. Read on and you'll see what we mean.

❦ An Urgent Fax ❧

Alicia Sheerin

A public relations professional with Gregory Communications in Ardmore, Pennsylvania. Alicia states that she must be very creative in persuading national entertainment and business journalists to return her calls. She is. She has a 95 percent success rate.

This fax gets right to the point and it gets the right results:

Fax Cover Sheet
Gregory Communications Inc.
17 West Athens Ave., Suite 200
Ardmore, PA 19003
(610) 642-8253   FAX (610) 642-1258

Date:	10/16/95
Pages:	1
To:	Eric Yaverbaum
Company:	Jericho Promotions
Fax Phone:	(212) 260-4168
From:	Alicia Sheerin
Subject:	Urgent!

Eric:

It's imperative that we speak as soon as possible. Please call me at (610) 642-8253.

Alicia

Authors' Comment: This is so easy to do that we recommend you give it a try. Alicia swears it gets great results.

❧ You Better Call—or Else! ❧

Alejandro Modena

A toy and sundries importer in Burlingame, California, Alejandro sent this faxable message that usually gets a response.

You may know where you are.

God may know where you are.

But if Alex doesn't know where you are,

then let's put it this way:

You and God better be pretty good friends!

❧ The Checkoff List ❧

Hal Becker

Author of Can I Have Five Minutes of Your Time?, *Hal Becker has been sending the following fax for the past 11 years and claims it works like a charm:*

Please place a checkmark beside the statement that best describes why you have not returned my call:

_____ You lost my message and forgot to call.

_____ You're just not interested.

_____ You think I'm an idiot and wish I would go away.

_____ Not returning my call is a power play, but, if I beg enough, you'll call me back.

☙ Something's Wrong ❧

Dr. Norman Lamm

President of Yeshiva University in New York, Dr. Lamm claims
his technique works very effectively.

First, I am always courteous. Most people return calls to "nice" people. But if I do not get called back after making four or five calls to somebody and leaving my name and number, I fax the following message:

> Dear _____:
>
> There must be something wrong with your phone system. After several repeated attempts to call you, I have not heard back from you. Please look into this.
>
> > Sincerely,
> >
> > Norman Lamm

❧ Just the Fax, Ma'am ❧

Margaret Torme

*Creative director at Torme & Kenney in San Francisco, Margaret sends
the following fax to people who don't return her calls:*

Facsimile Memorandum

To: Joe Doe
Fax: 999-9999
Pages: (1) including this cover page
From: Margaret Torme
Fax: 888-8888
Phone: 777-7777
Date: December 20, 1996
Re: Phone Tag

I'm sure there's a very good reason you haven't returned my call. I don't want to be a nuisance. So just fax back your response—or call me—and we'll take it from there.

_____ I'm out of town.

_____ I really don't want to talk to you.

_____ I'm busy on my deadline. Call me next week.

_____ Call me at _____ (time) on _____ (date).

_____ I no longer work here.

_____ I'm sorry. I really will call you soon.

_____ If it will take 10 minutes or less, call me now.

_____ Other (fill in): _____

Section Five

❧ Follow-up Letters, ❧ Surprise Packages, Etc.

Sometimes it's necessary to employ extra ammunition to get the job done. In this section, you'll discover what you can do with effective follow-up letters and even a few surprise packages to coax open those closed doors.

Included are some wonderful follow-up letters. Or, for even more immediate results, you can send a surprise package by messenger or overnight courier. And you may even want to try bombardment by a series or combination of letters and packages to supplement your phone calling and faxing campaign. This section offers some wonderful alternatives for generating results that a phone message alone cannot get.

❧ Instant Results ❧

Eric Yaverbaum

The coauthor used this ingenious and entertaining follow-up to snag an important new client. Remember that creativity almost always gets good results.

When the word hit the street that Club Med was looking for a new public relations firm, the company was swamped with publicists seeking the account. All told, my firm was one of a long list of 25. If the list was put in alphabetical order, with a name like Yaverbaum, I wouldn't even get to bat before the company made its choice.

I knew I had to come up with an innovative idea if I were to be in the running. From past experience, I knew a run-of-the-mill approach wouldn't do much good. It was imperative to make a first impression that conveyed the message, "Eric Yaverbaum is a creative, resourceful person." After all, if someone is looking for a public relations firm, an advertising agency, or, for that matter, any kind of consulting firm, isn't this the one image to immediately get across? After sleeping on it for a night, I came up with what I considered a winner.

I had a messenger deliver a big box to the vice-president that contained packages of instant oatmeal, instant coffee, instant pudding, instant mashed potatoes, instant glue, instant hair dye, one-minute nails, and a can of minute orange juice. In the box, I enclosed a handwritten note:

> By using these products, perhaps you will find an extra few minutes in your busy day to give me a call.

The next morning, the president called to set up an appointment for our firm to make a presentation to Club Med. We got the account.

Authors' Comment: We love this one, and it's something anyone can do in almost any situation. It demonstrates to the other party that you are creative.

❧ A Picture Says a Thousand Words ❧

Kathy Keenan

*Kathy (whose title on her business card reads "Empress of the Universe")
works with Oak Ridge Public Relations, Inc., in Cupertino, California.
Before starting a cold-calling campaign to drum up new business, Kathy came up
with an unusual—and effective—attention getter. The agency produced an
18×26-inch two-color poster and mailed it to prospective clients.
Empress Kathy explains the follow-up.*

The cartoon-illustrated poster recounts 14 moments in history and presents humorous examples of the do's and don'ts of public relations. Some examples from the poster:

> **38 A.D.:** Caligula had his horse, Incitatus, named to the Roman Senate. Due to shrewd image building, the election of Incitatus to the Senate was the first time in history that the front end of a horse occupied public office.

> **1776 A.D.:** The Revolutionary War. The Americans took to wearing earth tones and hiding behind trees to sharpshoot at the British. The guys in red coats with the nice white crosses on their chests were easy marks, proving that creative and unconventional tactics can win over superior firepower.

The posters were delivered in mailer tubes, one week before making our initial phone calls. Our firm's rate of returned calls increased dramatically from 10 percent to a whopping 90 percent!

> **Authors' Comment:** If you decide to use this technique, we recommend spending the few extra pennies to go first class. Don't cut corners by using a black-and-white reduced poster. And make sure it contains a clever message.

❧ You Just Won the Instant Lottery! ❧

David Armour

Upon graduating from Cornell University, David Armour started his job search in a most overcrowded profession: New York's highly competitive television production industry. What David did obviously worked. Today he is the supervising producer for The Ricki Lake Show.

Using my computer, I made up a Lotto card, putting my photo in all nine spaces. I had it printed in color, mounted on cardboard, and attached to tin foil. The card read:

> Your goal is to match three of the same pix—diagonally, horizontally, or vertically—and *you* win the prize!

The card was sent to the industry's top people, and I received responses from everyone, even producers who had no openings. One man called back to say, "We receive thousands of resumes and phone calls, and even though we're not in the market for somebody at this time, I had to contact you to meet the person who did this!"

> ***Authors' Comment:*** If this doesn't get you in the door for an employment interview, you're probably better off working somewhere else!

✎ The Big Fish ✍

Paul Barnett

A New York consultant on unemployment insurance for large companies, Paul was having difficulty getting to see an important prospect in the South.

When I finally got the guy on the phone, he said to me, "I'm sorry, but I don't have time to talk to you. *I have bigger fish to fry.*" And he hung up.

The next day, I had a $22 frying pan delivered to his office to help him fry his fish. He called me back the same day he received it to set up an appointment.

Two days later, we met and a contract was signed.

✑ The Big Boxes ✐

Joseph Sugarman

*Considered one of the best ad copyrighters in the United States. Here Sugarman
reveals a technique he used and a lesson he learned when he was a
26-year-old salesperson just out of the army.*

Back in 1965, when I was in charge of sales and marketing for Ski Lift
International, I sold ski lifts throughout the country. I had targeted 100 ski
resorts as prime prospects for my product, and it didn't take much time to place
calls to each of them. At one point, I had successfully made contact with 80
resorts, which resulted in the sale of one ski lift. It was a major job, and my company considered it a successful sales campaign.

There were 20 resorts, however, that I was unable to make any headway with,
no matter how many repeat calls I made. There must be another way, I thought. I
decided to employ a follow-up strategy incorporating a direct mail campaign
designed to arouse curiosity and ultimately lead to telephone conversations.

My plan was to send a personal note to each prospect and, with it, an
unusual gift. The first week, a large button with the message "No Jerk" went out.
It extolled the wonderful "no jerk" feature on our new T-bar ski lift. The second
week, I sent a folder that, when opened, expanded, and in large print read, E-X-
P-A-N-D, suggesting that my prospect expand his ski lift operation by purchas-
ing our latest model. Along with each mailing, I placed a personal call to the
decision maker. "Please tell Mr. Jones that the person who sent the 'No Jerk' button is on the phone," I'd say.

As my campaign began to dwindle to the sixth and final week, the number
of prospects who would not return my calls had shrunk to eleven. As the weeks
went by, I had fewer gifts to purchase, so I spent more money each week. The
gifts became more expensive, more elaborate, and bigger.

To arouse interest for week six, two large packages were sent: a box full of apples and a box full of oranges. My message would highlight the big difference between my product and my closest competitor: The difference was like apples and oranges.

Before this last mailing, I called each prospect's secretary and said, "My name is Joe Sugarman of Ski Lift International, and I have two large boxes to send to Mr. Jones. Could you tell Mr. Jones that I'm on the phone and need his home address?"

A funny thing happened. Ten of the eleven prospects personally got on the phone, congratulated me on my excellent mailings, and wanted to know what I was sending them. I assumed that their curiosity, heightened through the mailings, had finally overcome their resistance to take my call. These last eleven prospects (the eleventh called me later) turned out to be even more responsive than the previous ones on the list. One even hired me to do some of his advertising.

As a follow-up to this story, I wondered what would happen if I skipped all the previous gifts and called the secretary directly. So I called secretaries and said, "I need the home address of Mr. Jones because I have two big boxes to send him." To my surprise, almost every new prospect I called accepted my call. I had indeed discovered the ultimate tactic in the battle to reach my prospect.

✒ Send It in Concrete . . . ✒

Jack Gerken

President of Brighton Communications in Costa Mesa, California, Jack relates how his staff got through to actor Charlton Heston.

Back in the late 1980s, our client asked us to produce a spectacular event in honor of Hollywood's 100th anniversary called Hollywood II. Part of the festivities was a gala street party that shut down Hollywood Boulevard for a week. We had the Goodyear blimp, spotlights that lit up the sky—the whole nine yards. During the early planning stage, it was decided that we should invite some of the movie industry's biggest stars to participate in the event. We figured if we could get Charlton Heston to serve as our master of ceremonies, he would be a major drawing card attracting other Hollywood personalities.

Knowing that landing one of the biggest names in show business is always an incredibly difficult task, we figured that, unless we had something fantastic to arouse his interest, we'd be just another request to turn down. After a lengthy brainstorming session, we sent an invitation to Heston on a concrete scroll of the Ten Commandments. Its inscription included a request for him to serve as our master of ceremonies. It was shipped via Federal Express, and I understand it was one of the heaviest packages the company ever delivered.

Heston called back and said, "Anybody who goes to the trouble of sending an engraved Ten Commandments invitation—in concrete—must really want to have me there. I hereby accept your invitation to serve as master of ceremonies."

Authors' Comment: If this worked on Charlton Heston, it must be good!

❧ Oh, Fork! ❧

Artie Isaac

President of Young Isaac, an advertising, public relations,
and marketing strategies firm in Columbus, Ohio.

After several unreturned phone calls, some people receive a rather unusual letter from us. A manila envelope arrives at their office containing a sheet of our letterhead mounted on cardboard with a fork attached to it.

Below the fork is the message: "Oh, fork! We understand how busy you are, and we know you have a lot of things on your mind. All we want to do is take you to lunch and show you how we can help you."

The closing message: "Don't make us come after you with a knife."

Generally, people call us back immediately!

Authors' Comment: This is clever and sends a great message to a potential client: "This is the kind of firm you'd like to do business with."

❧ Send It Air Mail ❧

Ogilvy & Mather

The following method of getting a VIP to return a call has been used successfully by the legendary advertising firm Ogilvy & Mather at its New York offices.

A cage containing a live carrier pigeon is delivered by messenger with an attached note. It reads: "We were worried about you. You're not returning our calls. We want to find out if you are dead or alive. Let the bird go."

By the way, the pigeon actually carries the note back to its home, and the message is then delivered to the ad agency.

Authors' Comment: Of all the recommendations in the book, this may be the hardest to implement. But if you happen to have access to a carrier pigeon, it's tremendous!

❧ A Gift of Information ❧

Dennis Kimbro, Ph.D.

Author of Think and Grow Rich, A Black Choice. *Dennis lives in Decatur, Georgia, and is a lecturer for the Napoleon Hill Foundation.*

I have a philosophy that people don't care about you unless you care about them. Working on this premise, I like to fax articles or send books to people that might have an interest in them. Since I work on referrals, I ask a lot of questions to figure out people's interests. For instance, early in my career when I was applying for a job at Coca-Cola, I sent a little book on management to the vice-president of human resources with a note stating that I thought he might find it interesting. Upon receiving the book, he called me immediately and gave me the interview I wanted.

We live in an information-driven society, which means most people have jobs requiring them to become more and more efficient. Knowing this, it's easy to find an appropriate article or book that practically everyone can appreciate.

❧ The Subpoena ❧

Jeff Slutsky

Professional speaker and author. Headquartered in Columbus, Ohio,
he is the president of Street Fighter Marketing, Inc.

After placing several calls to a prospect and never getting a return call, I came up with a brainstorm. While visiting the office of my best friend—a deputy prosecutor—I eyed a pad of blank subpoena forms on his secretary's desk. I "borrowed" one and filled in the blank spaces with a warrant ordering the prospect to appear in my office. Another friend delivered it for me—in his SWAT team uniform.

The prospect nearly had a nervous breakdown when the subpoena was handed to him. He was so relieved to see it wasn't the real thing, he called me immediately to compliment me on my ingenuity and persistence. He has been a client ever since.

> ***Authors' Comment:*** Be sure to selectively pick someone when sending a subpoena. After all, scaring the daylights out of someone is a shaky way to begin a business relationship!

☙ Handle with Care ❧

Ritchie Lucas

A principal at CreatAbility, a national, multiethnic creative communications agency specializing in advertising, marketing, and public relations and based in Miami.

Inducing media people to cover a client's event, such as a product launch, is a constant challenge. To assure that our requests are answered and to capture the media's attention while garnering maximum coverage, we must do something different.

Our agency overcomes this hurdle by sending out a customized 3DPR® [canister] execution. Each time we do this, due to the creativity of the idea, we receive an enormous response. For instance, we recently sent out a mock biohazardous waste canister, complete with two orange warning labels. The canister contained slimy green gook *and* a laminated press release for our client's launch! The canister is delivered by biohazard "specialists" dressed from head to toe in white hazard suits! This generated return calls from an army of otherwise cynical journalists. It worked well because, in today's bottom-line, buttoned-down business world, people look forward to creative change. Who says that public relations has to be one-dimensional!

❧ Speed Dialing ❧

Eric Yaverbaum

Coauthor Eric Yaverbaum tells the following story.

Early in my career in public relations, I put in several calls to the director of public relations at Subway Sandwiches. At the time, we were a tiny agency, and Subway was not yet the huge success it is today.

After many futile attempts to speak with the director, I came up with an idea. I sent him a telephone that had a speed dial feature—a novelty at the time—and I programmed it so that my phone number was on every speed dial!

As a public relations agent, I wanted to impress him with my resourcefulness and creativity. Evidently it worked, because he returned the call and we got the account!

❧ Be My Beneficiary . . . ❧

Anonymous

A CEO of a Fortune 500 company, who wishes to remain anonymous, used the following approach when he was just starting his career.

For several months, our company was one of a dozen vying for the business of a giant manufacturer. No matter how many times my associates and I called Mr. Big, he refused to speak to us. Once while at the Pittsburgh airport, I was thinking about what I could do to get to this guy. I happened to walk by a Mutual of Omaha booth. So I impulsively bought a $500,000 flight accidental death life insurance policy naming Mr. Big as the beneficiary. The woman at the booth gave me a copy of the policy, which I sent to Mr. Big with a note saying, "Thinking of you." Two days later, he called to set up an appointment to see me.

> **Authors' Comment:** This is extremely clever. For the little money it costs, it definitely does the job.

❧ Making an Appointment by Mail ❧

Sindy Meltzer

Sales representative for DeVilbiss Health Care, Inc.
She lives in Exton, Pennsylvania.

After I took over a new sales territory, one of my accounts, which had experienced some problems with older DeVilbiss equipment years ago, refused to take my calls. So I wrote a letter that stated:

> I think it would be to your advantage to allow me to bring you up to date on new equipment that your company could benefit from using. I've been trying fiercely to contact you and have been extremely unlucky. My purpose for writing is to let you know I will be calling you on Monday at 9:30 and would like just five minutes of your time.

Evidently, he was impressed that I had respected his time enough to set up a telephone appointment, because his secretary was instructed to put my call through to him.

Authors' Comment: This is a conservative approach that cannot possibly offend anyone, and it should work with most people.

❧ It's a Bear ❧

Milton B. Suchin

Head of The Suchin Company in Valley Village, California, where he serves as personal manager for entertainers ranging from The Amazing Kreskin to Phyllis Diller. He also produces the Bill Harris "Cinema Spotlite" series for The Nostalgia Television Network.

Earlier in my career, I was getting a lot of receivers slammed in my ear when I called on big shots in the entertainment industry. To overcome their resistance, I purchased some plush teddy bears dressed in T-shirts with my logo on the front. I sent the bears to people with a note attached: "Bear with me. I just need a few minutes of your time."

They were amused, and my calls were returned. And believe me, if this works on directors and executive producers in Hollywood, it should work on just about anyone! The bears were so popular that today I still send teddy bears as Christmas presents to secretaries.

❧ Flying High ❧

Pat Burns

Founder and president of Pat Burns Seminars.
She lives in Newport Beach, California.

To create interest in hiring me as a speaker, I recruited my kids and friends to help "package" my message. We filled 273 latex balloons with helium, tied an eight-foot string to each balloon and attached a note with a message:

> A speaker to pick?
>
> No need to get sick,
>
> Pick up the phone and find out why,
>
> Working with Pat will leave you high.

Each balloon was placed in an 18×18-inch box and marked, "Highly Perishable—Open Immediately," and shipped UPS. When the box was opened, the balloon flew out!

Since helium is lighter than air, each box was light in weight, causing curious office personnel to be anxious for Mr. Big to open it. A day or so after the packages were delivered, I called and identified myself to the secretary as the sender of the package. Everyone knew who I was, and my calls were immediately put through!

❧ At Exactly . . . ❧

Rick Hill

*President of Hillbrand, a food supplements company headquartered
in Tucson, Arizona.*

Before I call a prospect, I send a handwritten, hand-stamped envelope and a letter stating that I would like to seek his or her opinion. I always add, "I will call you on Thursday, January 12, at exactly 3:22 P.M." I always select an odd minute during the hour rather than 3:00 or 3:30. This, I believe, gets people's attention because it is such a specific time.

When the gatekeeper asks, "What is the nature of your call?" I reply, "Mr. Jones is expecting my call at 3:22 P.M. Please tell him Mr. Hill is on the line." My singleness of purpose and focus on timeliness take the gatekeeper by surprise, and my call is put through.

It's possible, however, that Mr. Jones might be on vacation or a business trip, and the secretary replies, "He's out of town so he couldn't possibly be expecting your call."

In that case, I answer, "Really? I had written down to call him at exactly 3:22 P.M. When do you expect him to return?"

Then out goes another letter to him with still another preset appointment scheduled on a precise minute during the hour.

❧ The Plant ❧

Lezlie Campeggi

Sales representative for Arcus Data Security, Inc., in Dominquez Hills, California.

Several years ago, I was vice-president of marketing and sales for a company providing armored car and cash processing services. Like Brink's, we would pick up a customer's money and take it to the bank to be deposited. Without mentioning the company name, let me say it was owned by a prominent, high-profile Southern California family; its senior management consisted entirely of family members.

One of our company's particularly large accounts, which was headquartered in Seattle, had made a recent acquisition. We estimated the new subsidiary would generate additional annual revenues for our company in excess of $85,000. When the account was turned over to me, I eagerly looked forward to making a sales presentation to the newly acquired business.

When I identified myself to the secretary and asked for Betty Wilson (a fictitious name), I was told she wasn't available and would call me back. But Wilson never returned my calls, even though I called her on a weekly basis for six months.

She did, however, go over my head and talk to several of the family members. Each time, she told them, "I prefer to deal with someone who is an owner of the company. I don't want to deal with one of your underlings."

I guess it didn't matter to her that I held a vice-president's position with the company. I simply didn't have the right last name. To the family's credit, each time Wilson called, she was told, "Ms. Campeggi is the best qualified person to handle your account." Still, Wilson refused to take my calls.

Late one afternoon, I called her, and evidently her secretary had left for the day, because Wilson answered her own phone. "Well, hello!" I greeted her enthusiastically. "This is Lezlie Campeggi, and am I glad to finally have an opportunity to speak personally with you!"

It was not, however, a pleasant conversation. "I don't like the treatment I'm getting from your company," she said abruptly. "I've done business with the owners of your company for many years, and I don't appreciate being treated as a second-class customer!" And slam—she hung up on me!

That hurt! But after doing a slow burn, I calmed down. Being angry wouldn't accomplish anything, I reasoned. With this in mind, the following morning, I called a local florist that had a reputation for exquisite plants. I selected a large, expensive plant and overnighted it to her with a card and a handwritten message: "I hope you're having a better day than yesterday. If so, call me. Lezlie."

Evidently Wilson was touched by the gift, because as soon as the plant was delivered, she called me, raving about how much she appreciated it. Then she changed the subject. "What do you say we make an appointment to discuss setting up our new subsidiary with your services?" she volunteered.

Our branch manager in Seattle has since told me, "Every time I visit Wilson's office, she says, 'Look at this gorgeous plant Lezlie sent me.'"

Authors' Comment: Lezlie didn't pennypinch and send just a bouquet of flowers. She sent an expensive plant! With a potentially large account, you want to make a definite statement—which she evidently did!

❧ Red Tape ❧

Jennifer Becker

A real estate broker with Samuel & Associates, a shopping center developing firm with offices in Cleveland, Ohio, and Boston, Massachusetts.

For three days, I placed calls to the real estate department of a chain of retail stores. But I could never get through to the right person to discuss my proposal for the company to lease space in a shopping mall I represented. Without naming the store, I can say it was part of an international, multibillion-dollar conglomerate. That was part of the problem. The company was so big, it was riddled with bureaucracy. The switchboard kept transferring me from one department to another, from one executive to another.

When I finally identified the decision maker, I called him—and called him. I must have left a dozen messages, but he never returned my calls. So I sent him a big sloppy ball of red tape with this note attached:

> After all the red tape I had to go through to get to you, I'd love to meet with you in person to discuss a hot property available in one of our Michigan malls.

The same day my package arrived, he called to schedule an appointment to meet with me. His company has since leased stores in several of our malls.

Authors' Comment: This is an especially good approach to use with people who work for large companies—and the U.S. government!

❧ Back to the Future ❧

Joe H. Bourdow

*Executive vice-president of Val-Pak Direct Marketing Systems, Inc.,
in Largo, Florida.*

I began my career with Val-Pak as a franchisee in Richmond, Virginia. One prospect in particular would never call me back, no matter how many times I called him. It was annoying because I knew he needed our services. One day, in frustration, I sent him an unsolicited proposal in an elaborate binder. On its cover, I put down the date, January 1, 1995, five years into the future.

Shortly after he received it, he called. "Impressive proposal, Joe, but one comment. You dated it January 1, 1995. Why five years from now?"

"Because that's how long I figured it would take me to get through to you," I replied.

That was the door opener. He's been a client ever since.

❧ A Personal Touch ❧

James Dawson

Founder and president of Dawson & Associates, a marketing consulting firm in Lexington, Massachusetts. He is a past president of the American Marketing Association and the Business Marketing Association.

Shortly after the initial public offering of a hot company, I put in a call to the firm's vice-president of marketing. Needless to say, there was no shortage of phone calls going into that company!

After several unreturned calls, I sent him a greeting card with a beautiful Monet painting on its cover. Inside I handwrote a note telling him about my background, my creative director, and our company. Shortly afterward, he returned my call to arrange a date for us to make a formal presentation.

In this case, I happened to know he had an interest in art. I send cards with handwritten notes on a regular basis, most of them more novel and humorous, of course, depending on the client. Sending a card has a nice personal touch, which is what gets them to respond.

Section Six

❧ Great Voicemail Messages ☙

Like it or not, voicemail is the norm today. Never mind that recent surveys reveal that most customers don't like voicemail. Get used to it, because it's here to stay. So instead of dreading voicemail, learn to use it to your advantage.

Once you see how easy it is to leave proven, field-tested messages, you'll embrace voicemail as your ally. The following entries reveal how some innovative and intriguing ways to leave messages induce people to return your calls.

You can begin using some of these voicemail messages immediately simply by reading them as they appear in this book! Others may take some practice before you master them. At the very least, there's enough material in this section so that you'll never be at a loss for effective words when you hear, "At the sound of the beep. . . ."

Using the Negative to Generate a Positive Response

Elizabeth Graham

Public Affairs Director at Liberty Science Center in Jersey City,
New Jersey, Elizabeth provides this tidbit that was always effective for
her when she worked at a museum.

I had trouble getting the museum's curators to return my internal calls. They were always doing something that to them was of vast importance, and they were always too busy to call me back.

Consequently, I came up with a clever solution that worked like a charm. I'd leave them a voicemail message in which I read copy from a press release, saying it would be sent out very shortly. I'd always be sure it included some information that was completely wrong.

They were so horrified about my "mistake" that they'd always call back immediately with a correction. Once I had them on the phone, I'd also get whatever other information I needed from them.

Authors' Comment: You don't have to be in public relations to use this technique. With some ingenuity it can be tailor-made to fit your own needs.

❧ Mommy's Helper ❧

Kim Bayne

*President of wolfBayne Communications, a public relations and
Internet marketing consulting firm.*

Since I work out of my home in Colorado Springs, my five-year-old daughter, Kaitlyn, works by my side in the afternoons. While I work diligently at my large desk, my little girl dutifully colors pictures at her smaller desk and sometimes chats on *her* phone, a broken but real one! Once a day, the two of us routinely sit down in front of a computer and surf the Internet. Each week, we update Kaitlyn's very own home page on the World Wide Web.

Recently, after making several attempts to get an editor to return my call, I left the following message:

> Hello. This is Kim Bayne. That's B-A-Y-N-E with wolfBayne Communications. Please call me regarding the upcoming story you're writing on semiconductors. I have some changes you'll need to include.

When I didn't get a return call, I tried once again. Still no results. "Awww, nuts!" I declared, banging down the receiver.

"What's the matter, Mommy?" Kaitlyn innocently asked.

After I explained, my daughter suggested, "Maybe he just doesn't want to talk to you. Do you want me to call him for you?"

"Why not?" I thought.

I dialed the editor and again his voicemail came on. Now it was my little girl's turn.

> Hello. This is Kaitlyn Ruth Bayne. That's K-A-I-T-L-Y-N-R-U-T-H-B-A-Y-N-E with wolfBayne Communications. Please call Mommy about the story you're writing on train conductors. Please call her because if you don't, I think she's

going to be nuts. Please pick up your telephone and push the right numbers. [*She looked down at the phone and read the number.*] If you don't want to do that, go to my Web page on the Internet. [*She recited the Web address.*] Thank you. Good-bye.

Astounded, I asked, "Why did you tell him to go to your Web page?"

"Just put a message there and tell him what you want," Kaitlyn explained.

It was absolutely the fastest message I ever wrote. I quickly uploaded my daughter's knock-knock jokes and riddles to http:/www.bayne.com/wolfBayne/kaitlyn/ with a link to a short letter from me.

Later that same afternoon, the editor called me. "I've spent the last ten minutes howling over your Kaitlyn's Web site," he said enthusiastically. "It was so delightful to hear from her in the middle of a hectic work day. I can't wait to get home tonight and show her home page to my five-year-old son."

Authors' Comment: This high-tech approach still has a nice warm touch.

❧ "Instant" Poetry ❧

Robert Shook

Coauthor Robert Shook says not everyone can be incredibly witty all the time, always coming up with the perfect response on the spur of the moment. Fortunately, there are opportunities for you to create the impression that you are fabulously clever. This is especially true when you are leaving messages on a voicemail or answering machine.

I once called a celebrity who was in the market to hire an author to ghostwrite his life story and was greeted by the following recording:

> I'm either away or asleep,
> So whenever you hear the loud beep
> You have four minutes more
> To tell me the score;
> Talk a lot, because talk is so cheap!

At a loss for words, I quickly hung up. Then I took half an hour to compose the following response, and called back to record it.

> I hope I didn't wake you.
> Were you really asleep?
> It's 3 P.M. on Tuesday—
> What hours do you keep?
>
> I'm the ghostwriter you seek
> To do your book.
> For a blockbuster best seller,
> Call Robert L. Shook.

Later that afternoon, I received an enthusiastic call from the celebrity. "How did you ever come up with such a delightful, spontaneous poem?" he asked. He obviously thought I had composed it on the spot and concluded I was both creative and witty!

I urge you to create an "instant" poem the next time you reach a recorded message, poetic or not. It's a sure way to arouse interest and get your call returned.

> ***Authors' Comment:*** It doesn't take a rocket scientist to figure out that someone who has a poem on the answering machine is likely to think a message in verse is clever.

❦ The Incomplete Message ❧

Clinton Ford Billups, Jr.

President of CFB Productions, Inc., in Riverton, Connecticut. He is a personal manager for entertainers, as well as a television producer.

Did you ever receive a message on your answering machine that you played again and again, yet you couldn't understand what was on it? It drives you crazy, doesn't it? And it makes you curious too. With this in mind, I leave incomplete messages, and they always get returned.

> Bob, I just had a conversation with Eric Yaverbaum. By the way, my name is Clinton Billups and my number is 999-9999. Eric and I were discussing the new book that. . . ."

Then I hang up.

Authors' Comment: Think back to the last time you had an incomplete message on your answering machine. Chances are good that you returned the call.

The Wrong Address Gets the Right Results

Rich Knerr

Cofounder and president of Wham-O Manufacturing Company, the manufacturer of such wonderful products as the Hula Hoop Toy, the Frisbee Disc, and the Super Ball Toy. From Wham-O's headquarters in Acadia, California, Rich discusses a technique he used to get calls returned when his company was still in its infancy.

I'd call and leave a message on an answering machine stating, "Hello, Bill, this is Rich Knerr at 999-9999 calling. Joe King's address that you wanted is 1234 Main Street." Even though Bill didn't ask me for King's address, he does know 1234 Main Street is the wrong address. Almost everyone calls me back to give the correct address.

This also works when I say, "To answer your question, Joe King's wife's name is Betty," when it is really Alice *and* when he really didn't ask!

Authors' Comment: Most people are nice and will go out of their way to give you the right name (street, etc.).

❧ Very Unimportant ❧

Sy Presten

A publicist in New York, Sy has a simple one-liner that he claims always gets a return call.

"Hello, this is Sy Presten. My number is 999-9999. It's extremely unimportant that you call me."

Authors' Comment: This warm, soft sale approach works!

You Haven't Returned My Call, So You Must Be Interested!

Tony Parinello

*President of Parinello, Inc., a sales training and consulting firm in
San Diego, California. He is a professional speaker and the author of
Selling to VITO (Very Important Top Officer).*

When somebody doesn't return my calls, I leave this message on voicemail:

> This is Tony Parinello, and you probably recognize my voice by now. I take the fact that you haven't returned my call as a good sign. It tells me you must be interested in what you're hearing because you're probably the kind of person who would have had somebody call to tell me to get lost if you had no interest. And because you haven't done that, you can plan to see me on Thursday at 3:00. That's when I'll be in your office. Now you know what traffic is like at 3:00, and, since I have no other appointments downtown on Thursday, I'm making a special trip just to see you. Please . . . if you have no intention to meet with me personally, I'd appreciate it if you'd have somebody call me by noon on Thursday. Again, I'm looking forward to meeting you in person. Now, if you'd like to call me right away, during the next hour, here's the number where I can be reached.

I've left this message on the voicemail of some very important top officers (VITOs), and boy do they call me back pronto!

❧ I Guarantee That I'll . . . ❧

Jeff Gitomer

Author of The Sales Bible: The Ultimate Sales Resource.

After reading my book, a salesperson phoned me and said: "I would like you to call my boss and tell him to hire you to speak at our annual sales conference. You'll have to leave a message on his voicemail, though, because he's never in."

Sure enough, I called and got the voicemail. "This is Jeffrey and my number is 999-9999," I said. "You don't know me from a sack of potatoes, but one of your sales reps called me and said he wanted you to hire me to address your sales seminar. I want you to know that I guarantee to double. . . ." and I hung up.

Within four minutes, he returned my call. "Jeffrey, this is Steve. What's the rest of your message?" he blurted out.

"Steve, that was just a technique I use that I want to teach your salespeople when I speak at your annual sales meeting, so that they'll get all their phone calls returned."

"We've been looking for a speaker, and you're the guy we've got to have!" he answered.

❧ I'm Returning *Your* Call ❧

Anonymous

A CEO who wishes to be anonymous claims the following simple message works wonderfully on answering machines.

This is _____, and I'm returning your call. My number is 999-9999.

Busy people make so many calls, they don't remember whom they called! But if they called, they must have had a reason!

Authors' Comment: Take it from this anonymous CEO (who heads a Fortune 500 company): Most CEOs place so many calls, they truly don't remember whom they called and whom they didn't. Rather than checking it out, it's easier and quicker for them to make the call.

✒ Happy Birthday! ✑

Melinda Henning

Owner of a telecommunications company headquartered in Redwood City, California, that specializes in training sales and customer service people. She has written several books on telephone selling.

People are so busy today that, if you make a cold call to them, it will probably take several calls before you get a response. Knowing that busy people don't normally return calls to someone they don't know, I always leave a message on voicemail, figuring it takes at least five exposures before they recognize a new name. With this in mind, I prefer to call a small group of select prospects several times rather than call 100 people only once, who probably won't call back.

Once, after placing several calls to a San Francisco executive with a large international company, I heard the following outgoing announcement on her voicemail:

"It's my birthday and I'm taking a play day. Please leave a message." In response, I sang a beautiful and complete rendition of "Happy Birthday," and then left my number.

The next day she called back and said, "I'm so happy you kept calling because it was so much fun having you sing 'Happy Birthday' to me. You sound like someone I should do business with."

My persistence and singing resulted in a substantial order.

Authors' Comment: This has such a nice warm feeling, it's hard to imagine that someone would not respond.

❧ The Name Game ❧

Steve Lowe

Director of sales at Harrahs Lake Tahoe in Lake Tahoe, Nevada.

I use a play on my last name to draw attention to messages I fax to our customers. In large, bold print, one of my memos states: **"LOWE KEY REMINDER"** and another says **"LOWE PRESSURE SALES PITCH."** This gets people's attention and my calls are returned.

Authors' Comment: Of course, not everyone's last name is Lowe. But with a little imagination, this tip can work for a lot of us. Here are a few examples:

Name	Message
Sue Able	"I've left several messages. When will you be *able* to return my call?"
Bill Grant	"*Grant* me one wish and please return my call."
Fred Moore	"How many *moore* times do I have to call to talk to you?"
Ed Redd	"You haven't returned my call, and I'm starting to turn *redd*!"
Sam Shore	"For a *shore* thing, call me."

If your name isn't a "real" word, you can always write a cute poem. Here are a few examples of some common names:

Bill Brown	"Are your phone lines down? You haven't returned my call—Bill Brown."
Bill Green	"Is something wrong with your answering machine? When you get this message, call Bill Green."
Frederick Jones	"When you get this message on da phones, be sure to call Frederick Jones."

Brenda Lee	"I'm beginning to think you don't like me. Would you kindly call Brenda Lee."
Bob Miller	"For a story that's a real killer, call 999-9999—ask for Bob Miller."

Author Bob Shook likes this approach so much, he's now faxing the message, "You haven't returned my call, and I'm all *shook* up."

And author Eric Yaverbaum has since turned poet and faxes the following message: "To *tell* your fortune, read your palm. To *make* a fortune, call Eric Yaverbaum."

This is an interesting approach. Although we don't recommend it for everyone, we both tried it and can vouch it works well with certain people.

Section Seven

❧ Quickies ❦

The beauty of these techniques is that they're quick and easy. No faxing required. No sending letters or packages. Just simple one- and two-liners that do what they are supposed to do: get results. What's more, you can put them into action in a jiffy!

Mind Reading

Robert Shook

Coauthor Robert Shook claims that this approach works because it catches people off guard. After a brief pause to digest what you just said, the gatekeeper puts your call through.

"Good morning, Great American Corporation."

"Please put me through to Mr. Joe Green (company CEO)."

"Mr. Green's office. Susan speaking."

"This is Robert Shook calling. I want to speak to Joe Green."

"Does Mr. Green know the nature of your call?"

"Not unless he's a mind reader. Kindly put me through to him, Susan."

❧ Some Great One-Liners ❧

Wendy Basil

Executive vice-president of Halsted Communications in Los Angeles, Wendy submitted the following one-liners that she swears by. Halsted offices, through their Fleishman Hillard affiliation, are located around the globe. Their headquarters are in Ventura, California.

"I'll hold for him. I'm in the emergency room." Once I get through to him, I explain that my office *is* an emergency room!

"This is the State Franchise Tax Board calling." When the return call arrives, I explain, "I want to be one of your dependents."

"I have a question concerning the State Lottery." My follow-up is, "Have you ever played?"

"I need to talk to her today. I also have a call into [competitor's name], but I wanted to talk to her first."

"I'm calling because your name came up at a meeting, and I thought you would like to know what was said about you."

When a receptionist asks, "What's the nature of your call?" I reply, "I'm returning his call, so I don't know what we'll be discussing."

Authors' Comment: Choose the people who share your sense of humor. Just how effective these approaches are depends on your personality.

❧ I Plan to Proceed . . . ❧

Charlie Rath

Executive vice-president of marketing at Wendy's International, Inc., Charlie has been using the following line for years and claims, "It gets 'em every time."

Early in my career, through trial and error, I came up with a great line, and I've been using it on gatekeepers and leaving it on answering machines ever since. I simply say, "I plan to proceed as follows unless I hear from you to the contrary."

Authors' Comment: If it's true that curiosity killed the cat, then this approach is gonna kill 'em.

❧ Great News ❧

Lisa Lapides

Head of Lapides Publicity Group in Bingham Farms, Michigan, Lisa has a quick, direct approach that can be used in practically any situation.

When the gatekeeper asks, "What's the nature of your call?" I say, "Tell her I have great news!"

Who doesn't like to hear great news? People can't resist what I might have to tell them. When they get on the phone, their usual response is, "What's the great news?"

Of course, it's always easy to have something that I think is great news! Now whether *they* think it's great news is a matter of opinion!

Now and then, a gatekeeper asks, "What's the great news?"

"I can't tell you," I answer. "It would ruin the surprise."

Authors' Comment: This approach is great! It's so easy to do, we recommend you try it immediately.

❧ The Boss Said . . . ❧

Michael L. Lee

*Head of the Sales and Marketing Department of a high-tech company
in the San Francisco Bay area.*

I simply call the CEO's office and ask the secretary who I should speak to about what I'm calling for. Then I contact that party's secretary or leave a message on voicemail saying, "I was referred to you by Mr. Big's office." Note that I say Mr. Big's *office,* not Mr. Big, so what I am saying is true. It works like a charm. I get a high percentage of call-backs from the person I need to speak with.

～ Birthday Greetings! ～

Edward Lubin

The national syndicator of the Pat Boone Show, which is syndicated worldwide and based in Beverly Hills, California.

It's easy to find out someone's birthday. In the case of somebody important, you can look it up in *Who's Who.* You can also ask a secretary or business associate. Most people give you this information without resistance. Just say that you're going to send a surprise birthday present or that you're putting together an executive birthday directory.

Once you know the person's date of birth, call on that special occasion and tell the cross-examining gatekeeper, "I called to wish him a happy birthday." Believe it or not, the average executive gets only a handful of greetings on his birthday. So the gatekeeper thinks you're a personal friend and puts your call right through. Remember, too, that when you begin by wishing somebody a happy birthday, you automatically start off your call on a positive note.

Authors' Comment: This is so sweet and considerate, how could anyone hang up?

❧ Have You Heard the One about . . . ❧

Michael Craig

Michael books and manages seminars for his wife, Danielle Kennedy, a noted author and professional speaker. They reside in San Clemente, California.

I happen to be a terrific joke teller. So when I want somebody to return my call, I simply say, "Tell him I have a great joke to tell him!"

Since practically everyone enjoys a good laugh, my calls are almost always returned.

> ***Authors' Comment:*** For this one to work, you must have an ongoing relationship with the person you're calling. He or she must enjoy a good joke. The more serious, busy executive would probably not return your call!

⋙ The Out-of-Town Expert ⋘

Joe Gandolfo, CLU

The only life insurance agent in the world to sell in excess of $1 billion in a single year. A resident of Lakeland, Florida, Joe is truly one of the legends in the life insurance industry.

Since the vast majority of my clients are not in Lakeland, I'm constantly making long distance telephone calls. On a cold call, I simply say, "This is Joe Gandolfo calling from Lakeland, Florida. I'd like to speak to Frank Smith." There's no need to say anything more, because this may be all that's necessary.

However, a secretary may ask, "What's this in regard to, Mr. Gandolfo?"

"Financial planning" or "life insurance," I might reply.

Often, her response is, "He already has somebody locally who handles that."

"Ma'am, if there was anyone local who could do the job that I could do for him, I wouldn't be calling long distance," I say in a firm voice, "so I'll just hold." Then I remain silent and wait for Mr. Smith to come on the line.

Authors' Comment: Pulling off this real down-to-business approach takes a certain personality. So be careful with it: If your reply comes across as abrupt, you may turn off the gatekeeper.

❧ Something I Need to Ask You . . . ❧

Cindy Carney

An administrator at Paid Prescriptions Incorporated, headquartered in Parsippany, New Jersey, a division of Merck Pharmaceuticals.

A message that always gets my calls returned is one that I leave on voicemail: "There's something important I need to ask you. Please call me immediately."

Sometimes I'll be more specific, but not too specific. I'll say, "There's something important I need to ask you regarding the financial files." (You can fill in the rest of the sentence with a message that relates to the nature of your call.)

> ***Authors' Comment:*** Cindy claims that this technique is a winner because the "power of intrigue" is working for you. The person is riddled with curiosity about your question. Second, Cindy believes that people feel important when someone else needs information from them and them alone. This compels them to want to help by answering the "important" question. Cindy advises, "The less information left on the answering machine, the more intriguing it is." She says this technique always gets a quick response.

❦ The Hero Approach ❧

W. Randall Jones

CEO of Worth *magazine, headquartered in New York City. At age 30, he was the publisher of* Esquire—*the youngest publisher of a major magazine in U.S. publishing history.*

First, I send a compelling letter to get Mr. Big's attention. In the letter, I give an exact time and date when I will be calling him.

Then I make sure to call him at that precise time.

"What's it in reference to?" the gatekeeper may ask.

"It's in reference to making him a hero—an even bigger hero than he already is," I reply.

I usually get a warm reception when Mr. Big gets on the line.

Authors' Comment: This is a warm, friendly technique that is certain to win friends and influence people.

❧ The Referral ❧

Jay Bernstein

A legend among Hollywood agents, Jay is a master at getting telephone calls returned.

I like to use the name of a third party. The assumption is that the person I'm calling doesn't want to be on the you-know-what list of the third party. If I'm calling a producer, for instance, I might say, "I'm calling at the suggestion of Tom Cruise," or perhaps Julia Roberts. I'm well aware that the producer knows the person. There is no way he'll want to blow me off and as a consequence offend that person.

> ***Authors' Comment:*** If you don't happen to be into the Hollywood scene, you can always use the name of a local bank president, the mayor, or your congressional representative.

Section Eight

❧ Confusion, Innuendo, ☙ and Subtle Subterfuge

Over the centuries, to catch their enemies off guard, the generals of this world have employed confusion as their weapon. Likewise, callers can use confusion because, like experienced military leaders, the element of surprise is their ally.

In this section, you'll observe how innuendo can get you past even the most hardnosed gatekeeper and into the office of a high-ranking VIP. And, yes, there is even a place for subtle subterfuge.

A word of caution: Unless you fully master these techniques, you may occasionally find yourself treading dangerous waters. Even the most skillful specialists who routinely employ subterfuge end up with egg on their face once in a while, because a few people find it offensive or deceitful. For the record, on rare occasions, we feel there is a place for such tactics, but extreme discretion is advised.

❧ It's About the Money ❧
You Owe Me . . .

Charles Brotman

Head of his own public relations firm in Washington, D.C., Charles tells how he was able to get through to a client who owed him several thousand dollars.

I left message after message, but Mr. Jones never returned my calls. After two weeks of this, I was desperate. What could I do to make contact with him? How could I at least talk to him to work things out? I called him one more time and said, "It's urgent!" Still no return call.

Several times the receptionist had said he was on another line, but, after holding for what seemed like hours, I was told Mr. Jones wasn't in the office. Obviously, he didn't want to talk with me under any circumstances.

I began thinking it through: If it was someone other than me, he'd probably return the call.

This thought prompted me to have my secretary call and ask for Mr. Jones. When the receptionist asked who was calling, my secretary replied, "It's personal."

I can only imagine what went on while my secretary was on hold:

"Mr. Jones, there's a woman on the phone, but she won't give her name."

"Well, what does she want?"

"She said it was personal."

It must have been out of sheer curiosity that he responded. "Hello, Jones here. How may I help you?"

I'm sure he expected to hear a sweet voice on the other end of the line. But he got me instead.

"Hi there, Mr. Jones. This is Charlie Brotman. I know how busy you must be, not being able to return my telephone calls, but about the money you have outstanding with my company. . . ."

He was in such shock that he readily admitted he owed the money, apologized, and offered to mail me a check.

"Mr. Jones, I don't want to put you to all that trouble. I'm going to be in the neighborhood tomorrow morning. So I'll just pick up the check."

It worked!

I've used this tactic on two other occasions, and it worked brilliantly both times.

P.S. Be sure the woman making the call sounds "really nice."

Authors' Comment: When people owe you money, they have no right to complain that you "tricked" them into talking to you. After all, they shouldn't be hiding from you in the first place!

❧ You Leave Us No Choice ❧

Anonymous

*The following story was submitted by the owner of a small lamp manufacturing
company who was trying to collect a debt from a furniture store.
He requested that we do not use his name.*

Nearly five months had passed, and, despite sending several notices, I had still not received payment on a past-due invoice. It was a small order for ten lamps, and the invoice was only $350. Regardless of the amount, the money was owed, and I wanted to collect it.

At that point, I decided to call the owner personally, but when I identified myself, I was given the runaround. This happened a number of times. Each time, I was told that he was with a customer and that he would call me back. But he never did.

Finally, I had to do something to move the situation along. The last time I called, when the receptionist told me he wasn't available, in a burst of inspiration, I said, "I'm sorry, but he leaves me no alternative. My company has no choice but to take further action."

Amazingly, those words worked like magic.

"What do you mean?" the receptionist asked.

"I'm sorry, but I'm not at liberty to say," I replied. "This is a matter between your employer and me."

"Let me see if I could get him to come to the phone," she said. "I can see him from my desk, and I think he's just finishing up."

Two minutes passed, and the owner picked up the line. "No further action is necessary," he said. "I'll send you a check this afternoon."

Two days later, my mail contained his check for payment in full.

I can't even imagine what the secretary and owner thought I would do, but the truth is that, with small invoices of $350, my "further action" is usually to put the invoice into my uncollectible file and forget about it. My legal fees to collect on a small invoice are too high.

I've since used this line many times, and for some reason, people seem to get very nervous at being told further action will be taken against them. Not only do they call me back when I use this phrase, they send me the money due me!

Authors' Comment: The more we thought about it, the more we thought about how we would react if confronted with: "My company has no choice but to take further action." It's a subtle threat that isn't easy to ignore. It will work for a past due invoice in any field. It's also a great line for an attorney to use.

❧ A Pretty Voice ❧

Jim Clayton

*Chairman of the board and CEO of the Knoxville–based Clayton Homes, Inc.,
one of the largest manufactured-home companies in the United States.
Earlier in his career, as an attorney, he used the following method to
get through to delinquent clients.*

My secretary called the client and said in an intimate voice, "Tell Mr. Big this is Janie."

That's usually all it took to get Mr. Big on the phone. And when the gate-keeper asked the nature of the call, Janie replied, "It's personal," and she'd coyly add, "It's been quite a while, but he should remember."

It's amazing how a man reacts to a young lady who intimates that she's part of his past!

Then, once Mr. Big called back, Janie said in a sweet voice, "Thank you very much for returning my call. I'm with Mr. Clayton and he would love to chat with you." Then I'd quickly get on the phone before Mr. Big had a chance to hang up.

Authors' Comment: While Jim Clayton tells how his secretary called his male clients, a female executive can use the same technique by employing her male secretary to call on a female client. After all, women enjoy a sexy male voice.

❧ Calling for Liz ❧

Chen Sam

Headquartered in New York City, Chen heads her own public relations firm, Chen Sam & Associates. Her clients range from Elizabeth Taylor to Donald Trump.

When I'm asked to leave a message, I say, "Elizabeth Taylor is calling." Everyone returns my call. Even Hillary Clinton once did! Of course, since I've been representing Ms. Taylor for several years, I feel comfortable saying this.

> ***Authors' Comment:*** If you represent a VIP, we highly recommend this excellent approach. But we don't advise using your VIP clients' names unless your call relates directly to them.

❧ The Replacement ❧

Suzanne Carabelli

*A program consultant at Leading Authorities,
a Washington, D.C.–based speaking bureau.*

For more than a year, I put in a monthly call to John Smith, who was in charge of planning meetings for a large association based in Washington. During this period, I never got a booking with him or, for that matter, a return call. Sometimes, all I did was leave a message to say hello, tell him that if he ever needed me, I was here to serve him, and so on. Finally, one day out of the clear blue sky, he returned my call to tell me he was leaving the company. After I thanked him for his call, he replied, "My replacement is Mary Jones. You ought to give her a call after November first when I'm out of here."

On cue, I called her and said:

> I've been working with Mr. Smith for the past year, and I'm going to miss him. We had such a wonderful relationship. Now I understand that you're planning to have a speaker for your annual conference scheduled in the spring. I'd like to work with you on it, because I have some excellent speaker candidates for you.

The next day, she called me to book a speaker, and, ever since, I've used this technique in similar situations. Persistence and creativity definitely pay off!

❧ The Boss ❧

Anonymous

The following story was submitted by a rancher in Texas who wants to remain anonymous. Its method should work in many situations when calling on government employees.

I put in several calls to my congressperson, but none were returned. During my last call, an aide asked, "Who's calling?" I told the aide, "Tell him it's his boss."

"Who?"

"I said it's his boss."

I suppose the aide said, "Your boss is on the phone." As the congressperson came to the phone, he probably thought, "I've got to find out who this is—this person who thinks he's my boss!"

"Who is this?" he demanded.

"I'm your boss!" I insisted. "I'm a taxpayer, and therefore you work for me!"

After a brief silence, he said he had to admit I was right.

❧ Who's Calling Whom? ❧

Patrick Bresnan

Director of marketing of Bresnan Communications, headquartered in White Plains, New York. The company, which serves an estimated 180 communities throughout the United States, also has operations in Chile and Poland.

Every now and then, when I'm calling somebody and the secretary asks who's calling, I give the boss's surname. For instance, if I am calling Bill Shickman, I say, "Tell him Pat Shickman called. My number is 999-9999." She figures he must know me and no questions are asked.

This does not work, however, with a common name like Smith or Jones. But it is an excellent technique for a not-so-common name. Some people call back because they think it might be a long-lost relative, others because they're just intrigued and feel a kinship with someone who shares the same unusual last name.

Of course, I tip off my secretary to put through Shickman's call. Then, when I hear, "Hello. Pat Shickman?" I say, "No, this is Pat Bresnan. I called you this morning."

In a state of confusion, he'll say, "But my secretary said. . . ."

"Oh, she must have gotten the message confused because I called to tell you. . . ." Once I have him on the line, I feel as though I'm halfway home.

Authors' Comment: You should practice this technique before trying it. It can look easier than it really is.

Section Nine

❧ Charming the Gatekeeper ❧

One of the most common and effective approaches used by salespeople is extending their charm to the gatekeeper. Believe us, when this technique works, it indeed works like a charm. In this section, you'll see how some of the masters do it with ease.

There is a flip side, however. So many salespeople try this approach that, when it is done clumsily, gatekeepers are on to it in a flash. Refrain from over-doing it; don't lay it on too thick or it will backfire.

Since it's always a plus to have the gatekeeper as your ally, no matter what approach you use, remember that friendliness and charm go a long way. And never—absolutely never—be disrespectful to a gatekeeper. Someone who treats a gatekeeper like a doormat has only one opportunity to do so! Let your good-will and courtesy make your call a bright spot in a gatekeeper's day. Only then can you see how powerful gatekeepers are in getting you through to your party.

❧ Selling Yourself to the Gatekeeper ❧

Mary Kay Ash

Founder and chairman emeritus of Mary Kay Cosmetics Inc., a company with retail sales exceeding $1.5 billion. She is the author of the best-selling book Mary Kay, You Can Have It All.

Getting through to a top executive is difficult, but usually the secretary holds the key. Knowing that I must first win over this person, I recommend sending a gift or, better yet, personally delivering it. Anything from flowers to a box of candy will do. By being courteous and friendly, you'll eventually get the secretary on your side.

Then ask for an opinion: When is the best time to see the boss? Let us say she or he suggests that you call at 3:00. Ask to be put down as a telephone appointment for 3:02 or 3:03. This lets the boss know that you place a high value on every minute of his or her time—and yours. Finally, make sure you take only the time that has been allotted to you. This improves your chances of getting a follow-up call!

❧ Charming the Secretary ❧

Allan Armour

President of PSI Video in New York City, Allan advocates being friendly with a prospect's secretary and switchboard operator.

They hold the key to putting your call through. I use my charm to win over secretaries. Then I'll ask, "What do you recommend as the best time for me to call back? Do you mind checking Mr. Smith's calendar to see when that might be?"

A few moments later, you get the reply, "Hey, Al, call at 3:00 this afternoon. I know he's free then."

I've also been known to send out a box decorated with a Chinese design and containing two fortune cookies. One cookie has this message inside: "A great fortune awaits you." The other says, "Call Al Armour."

❧ Taking an Offensive Position ❧

Bernard Gross

*Not yet 30, Bernard already is a successful venture capitalist with
Paramount Capital in New York City.*

When the secretary of a high-profile executive asked the nature of my call, I replied, "It has to do with supporting medical research through a private placement in a public company." It was true, since I wanted to talk to him about investing in a biopharmaceutical company, an up-and-coming firm that was doing interesting things in drug research. This approach had opened many doors with other prospects.

Although his secretary, Kathy, took my message, Mark Smith didn't return my call. A few days later, I called again. After a brief conversation with his secretary, I left a second message, but still received no return call.

Every fourth day, I called Smith again. Each time, I was friendly with his secretary, and she extended the same friendliness to me. But there was still no return call. After two weeks, I continued calling to leave my name and number, but I stopped leaving a message. Sometimes Kathy and I chatted about the weather or even about her garden—nothing business-related.

Then I surprised her with a call I knew would get a reaction. "Kathy, I am shocked . . . ," I said and paused for her to respond.

"Shocked?"

"Yes, I'm sure Mr. Smith is a decent person, and certainly he's the type of person who returns phone calls. So I am shocked that he would be so arrogant and snobbish as not to return *my* calls. What is it? Is he just super busy? Does he actually plan to get back to me?"

Kathy was such a nice person, I could sense her embarrassment. "Let me see what I can do," she said apologetically.

Early that evening as I was clearing my desk, my phone rang. "Bernard, this is Mark Smith. Can you hear me? I'm in my car and I'm getting some static. I'm embarrassed that I've been so busy. . . ."

Obviously, my message had put him on the defensive. "I'm not the type of person who doesn't return calls," he apologized.

I believe I was able to get through to him as a result of the rapport I developed with his secretary. Once she and I were in harmony, I was able to be frank with her and express my feelings about her boss's behavior. Incidentally, Smith is a client of mine today—and my good friend.

> ***Authors' Comment:*** Once you win the confidence of warm-hearted gate-keepers, they will stand by you.

❧ My Boss Is Depending on Me ❧

Todd A. Koerner

An agent with the Writers and Artists Agency in Los Angeles.

I had made several calls to a big Hollywood producer on behalf of an actor I represented. Each time, his assistant said, "I'll take your number and he'll call you back," but the producer never did.

Finally, I said to her, "Look, I'm just doing my job, and every time I make a call to your office, I have to report back to my boss and let him know I couldn't get through."

"I'm sorry but . . . ," she apologized.

Recognizing that I had softened her up, I added, "My boss is depending on me to get through to your boss. And if I don't, he's not going to be happy with me."

Evidently, my appeal aroused her willingness to do a good deed for me. She probably identified with my plight, because, after all, she had to please a boss too. The producer called me back shortly afterward.

Putting the Gatekeeper on Your Team

W. Randall Jones

CEO of Worth *magazine, headquartered in New York City. At age 30, he was the publisher of* Esquire—*the youngest publisher of a major magazine in U.S. publishing history.*

Befriending the gatekeeper is paramount. When I'm told, "He's not in," I'll quip, "He's got some nerve! Didn't he know I would potentially be calling? Can't he read great minds?"

This generally evokes a laugh and warms people up. This is when I add, "You sound so wonderful. How long has 'Mr. Big' had you running his life?"

And if they sound really terrific, I say, "Let me tell you, if you ever think about prying yourself away from 'Mr. Big,' boy, do I have a position for you!"

I *always* get my calls returned with this last line. Several persons have called to see if I was serious. Of course, I'm serious!

I'll also challenge the gatekeeper with this line: "I'm willing to bet he won't return my call." Invariably, that gets my call returned!

❧ A Special Message to ❧ All Gatekeepers

Jim Throneberry

President of JET Advertising. Based in Colorado Springs, Colorado, his firm provides advertising and marketing consulting services to small and midsized companies. He frequently addresses audiences on the subject of telephone etiquette.

Gatekeepers typically ask a few questions. Sometimes—in frustration or to prove a point—I give them the following answers:

Gatekeeper:	Who shall I say is calling?
Reply:	Me.
Gatekeeper:	Can you spell that?
Reply:	Yes, I can.
Gatekeeper:	Who are you with?
Reply:	I'm with me.
Gatekeeper:	And what do you want?
Reply:	I want to talk to Mr. Jones.
Gatekeeper:	And where are you from? [*Translation:* What company do you represent?]
Reply:	Colorado Springs.
Gatekeeper:	What is the nature of your call?
Reply:	To talk to Mr. Jones.
Gatekeeper:	May I tell him why you are calling?
Reply:	Yes, you may.

Gatekeeper:	Will he know what this is in regards to?
Reply:	Only if he's a mindreader.
Gatekeeper:	And this is regarding? [*Or:* And this is pertaining to?]
Reply:	Yes, it is.
Gatekeeper:	Mr. Jones is not available. Is there someone else you would like to talk to?
Reply:	Sure. Who else is there?
Gatekeeper:	And what *was* your name?
Reply:	Well, it *still* is Throneberry, but I have been thinking about changing it.

So what should a gatekeeper say? My advice to all gatekeepers is to answer the phone as follows: "Good morning. XYZ Company. This is Jim."

Then, after the caller tells you whom or what he wants, pick a common sense answer:

> "Mr. Jones is on the phone [in a meeting, etc.]. May I have him call you?"
>
> "Is there any way I can help?"
>
> "May I leave him a message?"
>
> "May I tell him who's calling?"

My advice to all bosses: Your telephone is your lifeline and the first impression of your businesss. Don't let the person on the phone present a poor image of you or your company. Another thing: Whoever picks up the phone "owns" that call until the caller is satisfied.

Section Ten

❧ Good Advice ❧

"Good advice? What have I been reading?" No doubt you are thinking this.

Of course, we believe this entire book is filled with good advice. But, rather than dwelling on technique, this section is packed with specific tips that we think are just plain, old-fashioned good advice. Turn the page to see what we mean.

Matthew Lesko

A consultant in Kensington, Maryland. For more than 20 years, Matthew has made his living selling free government information to business clients for tens of thousands of dollars or repackaging it into books that have sold nearly two million copies.

Just give me a telephone. I believe that, no matter what information is needed, I can place an average of seven phone calls and probably find it somewhere in the government.

Over 37 percent of the entire U.S. economy is government. It has more information on subjects than anyone else in the world, and in most cases it has better information than anyone else. Consider this: The government spends $3 billion counting all the noses and toilets in the United States because the Constitution says we have to know how many Congressional representatives we should have. It's called a census, a marketing study that even General Motors couldn't afford.

Or think of this: Each year all U.S. publishers publish a total of 50,000 titles. But one little publisher in the government called the National Technical Information Service alone publishes over 100,000 titles a year, and no one has ever heard of them! The government has more computerized databases than all the on-line services combined, and the Internet would not be here today if it wasn't for the government, with special thanks to the U.S. Department of Defense!

Early in my career, a single phone call convinced me that the government was an information gold mine. That's when a client said that he needed to get basic information on the supply and demand for Maine potatoes—within 24 hours. He represented a syndicate of commodities investors who figured this information would provide them an edge over other investors. Just two telephone calls later, I was talking directly to Charlie Porter, an expert with the U.S. Department of Agriculture who held a masters degree in agricultural economics. For the past 14 years, Charlie had been studying the supply and demand of potatoes!

Charlie was terrific. We chatted for two and a half hours, and there wasn't anything he didn't know about the supply and demand of potatoes. He was a wealth of knowledge, spouting facts from hundreds of books he had read about potatoes. Charlie told me he had designed computerized models forecasting the supply and demand for potatoes. He received hourly updates giving him the price of potatoes in seven regions around the country. Once started, it was hard to stop him. I had a feeling that I was the first person who cared about his work. The government had probably forgotten he was there, and his wife was surely sick of hearing him talk about potatoes!

The government has a Charlie Porter–type expert on everything, and they're available to anyone for the price of a telephone call. The nicer you are on the telephone, the better your chances of getting your call back and getting all the information you need. That's not always an easy chore, because it's often frustrating and draining to be put through the bureaucratic runaround looking for your Charlie Porter. So don't take out your frustrations on him when you do finally talk to him: He's dying to help you.

Here are ten tips on how to talk to him or her:

1. Be cordial and cheerful. Make sure your call is a pleasant interlude in his or her day.

2. Be open and candid. Don't be evasive or deceitful in explaining your needs.

3. Be optimistic. Don't start off by saying, "You probably aren't the right person," or "You probably don't have what I need." It's too easy for the person to reply, "You're right."

4. Be humble and courteous. Experts love to tell others what they know, as long as their role as an authority isn't questioned or threatened. If you treat them with respect, you're likely to get even more information than you asked for.

5. Be concise. State your problem clearly and don't be long-winded.

6. Don't be a "gimme" (a person who says "give me this" and "give me that").

7. Be complimentary. A well-placed compliment about your source's expertise or insight goes a long way.

8. Be conversational. It's okay to talk about a few irrelevant topics ranging from the weather to the Washington Redskins. The more social you can be without being too chatty, the more likely it is that your source will open up to you.

9. Return the favor. You might share some information or even gossip you have, but be careful not to leave the impression that you have betrayed the trust of others.

10. Send thank you notes to assure that your source will return your calls and be just as cooperative in the future.

❧ Two Tips on How to Get ❧ Unlisted Addresses

Richard Lamparski

Author of a series of books entitled What Ever Happened To?, *Richard offers two suggestions on how to get addresses and phone numbers of celebrities.*

1. Addresses are available at the voter's registration office, which is open to the public.
2. If the spouse of a celebrity dies, you can go to the coroner's office. The next of kin and his or her address are registered there, and the information is available to the public.

Once you have an unlisted address, you can mail an effective letter that merits a response.

❧ Tips from a *National Enquirer* ❧ Senior Editor

Brian Williams

Senior editor at the National Enquirer.

I have three pointers that work well for me with the gatekeeper:

1. Make sure you know the first name of the gatekeeper and the person with whom you wish to speak. Then say, "Jill, it's Brian for Todd," and shut up. The chances are good that she'll put you right through. If she asks, "What's the nature of your call?" simply answer, "He'll know," and again be quiet.

2. Leave a strong but incomplete message. "Tell him it's Brian Williams, Senior Editor of the *National Enquirer.* I want to provide him with some information regarding a story we're about to publish." Note that I am *providing* information, not asking for it!

3. Call your party at home, then feign surprise that it is not an office number. "Oh, I'm sorry! Isn't this your office number?"

Here are three more tips that work well when leaving messages on an answering machine:

1. Some people screen calls before answering. When I suspect this, I say in an assertive manner, "Bob, it's Brian. Pick up." Then I play a waiting game and remain silent. Notice that I don't ask, "Are you there?" That question would make Bob feel sneaky. Given a face-saving assumption, people generally pick up the phone and talk to you.

2. I always repeat my phone number twice and very slowly. It can be a chore for some people to write down a phone number from an answering machine, particularly busy people with a lot of messages. I like to make it easy to call me back!

3. I like to leave a tantalizing message. I'll say, "This is Brian Williams from the *National Enquirer*, and I want to read to you what I am writing about you before we publish. But I need to hear from you by 3:00 this afternoon." I believe a definite deadline is essential. It creates urgency.

❧ Nice Guys Do Finish First ❧

Pat Williams

General manager of the Orlando Magic basketball team.

In my early days in sports management, my mentor was Bill Veeck, a legend in baseball who once owned the St. Louis Browns, the Cleveland Indians, and the Chicago White Sox. Veeck taught me a lifelong habit and a good one: Never screen your calls. "Take them yourself, Pat," he'd say, "and let the public have access to you." So for 30-some years, I have never screened a call.

Sometimes I encounter secretaries who think their job is to serve as a pit bull protecting a sacred boss! These persons like to ask four questions:

1. Who's calling?
2. What company are you with?
3. What is the nature of your call?
4. Will Mr. Big know who you are?

However, no matter how much these questions annoy me, I'm always pleasant and I simply leave my name and number. Just as I return every call, I expect others to extend the same courtesy by returning mine.

If I'm not in when somebody calls, I always make it known that I welcome the call. To accomplish this, I make sure to leave a friendly message on my answering machine, and I continually revise my message.

Authors' Comment: When the authors called Pat, his answering machine had the following message:

Hi, this is Pat Williams. Thank you for calling and a very merry Christmas to you. I get such delight watching my children hanging up their stockings

Christmas eve. It's not that it's Christmas eve. It's just such a thrill to see them hanging anything up!

Please leave your message. This is a confidential machine, and I will get back to you as soon as possible. Do me a favor: Leave your phone number twice. This is really important because I am trying to record these phone numbers in my Franklin Planner, and if you don't give it to me twice, there's a good chance I'll never get it copied down. So do that for me, and I will get back to you. By the way, if we look at it realistically, the Christmas presents of today are the garage sales of tomorrow. See you later. Bye-bye.

❧ The Right Thing to Do! ❧

Spencer Christian

Cohost and weatherman on ABC's Good Morning America, *Spencer told us this warm story with a message from which we all can learn.*

My demanding schedule with *Good Morning America* requires me to be on the road two days a week. This translates into lots of calls on my voicemail to return.

One message was left by a school teacher. She started by saying, "I know that you must get requests all the time and from all over the country. I'm sure that your schedule is very busy."

A lot of messages start out this way, but then she switched gears and played on my sympathy and desire to be a good guy.

> I've heard such nice things about you, Mr. Christian, and everyone says you enjoy giving your time to community service. I also know that you really love kids. And if you really love kids as much as I'm *told* you do—and if you really care as much about education as I'm *told* you do—I think you might decide to come to our school to speak to the students in my class.

Now how could I say no to this request? There was no way I was going to ignore this call. I called her right back and said:

> You know, ma'am, you have reaffirmed what I would like to believe about myself. So, in order for me to continue to feel good about myself, I have to say yes. I'll be delighted to speak in your classroom.

I could easily have passed this message along to an assistant who would have politely told the teacher my schedule was booked. But this teacher's appeal was aimed right at my heart. I had to call her personally to accept her invitation.

❧ The Perils of Not Returning Phone Calls ❧

Ken "Dr. Fad" Hakuta

The mastermind behind the Wacky Wall Walker, the sticky octopuslike toy of the 1980s. He earned his MBA at Harvard and now resides in Washington, D.C.

In the late 1980s, I became fascinated with Shaker furniture, which was designed and built by members of the Christian sect called the Shakers. Dating back to 1774 when the sect came to America to escape religious persecution in England, the Shakers shunned the outside world to pursue a plain and simple way of life. Their furniture reflected a stripped-down esthetic whose symmetry and simplicity were based on utility. I suppose it was my interest in American folk art that attracted me to become a collector.

A few years ago, I received a call from the Darrow School, a small school in Mount Lebanon, New York, built on the original site of the Shaker community. Due to financial difficulties, the school was selling off what was considered the definitive collection of Shaker furniture. Prior to calling me, however, they tried to contact renowned TV star and comedian Bill Cosby, who had once purchased an 1820s cupboard for $200,000 from the school. After making many calls to his office without getting a return call, they attempted to get his home phone number, but without success. Eventually, they gave up, and that's when they called me.

After a brief conversation with them, I visited the school and snapped up the entire collection for $600,000. The collection was recently appraised at over $3 million.

All I can say is thank heaven Bill Cosby never returned their calls!

Authors' Comment: An unreturned phone call can be very costly. We recommend that you make a copy of this story and, when the occasion is appropriate, fax it with a personal note to a person who is "too busy" to return your call!

❧ Opportunities Waiting to Happen ❧

Russell Cooper

*Located in Buffalo Grove, Illinois, Russell is a global account executive
with Federal Express.*

I'll never forget the valuable lesson I learned from one of my accounts. The company had an unusual written rule. As a senior manager told me, "Every person in our company, from the CEO on down, is required to return a call from a vendor before or by the fifth call."

"Why so?" I asked.

"Because otherwise, opportunities will be missed. We feel vendors are an extension of our staff. And if you're not talking to new vendors, you're failing at your job as a businessperson!"

Authors' Comment: Vendors and salespeople are wonderful sources of information. Successful people understand this and view them as "partners."

Be Sure to Call the *Right* Person

Steve Allen

One of America's favorite entertainers and a noted author,
Steve offers the following advice.

Since I am literally besieged by calls every day, it's not possible for me to talk to everyone who calls. I simply don't have the time. I'm least likely to return a call from a stranger who leaves only a name and number.

Without a clue to the nature of the caller's business, I see no reason why I should return the call. Ordinarily, however, members of my staff give callers the courtesy of a response, in which case they may say, "Could you please give us some hint, sir, of exactly what it is you're calling Mr. Allen about?" In most instances, it turns out I'm not even the right party to talk to. The caller is better served by speaking to my attorney, my business manager, my booking agent, my secretary, my music publisher, or another of my associates.

Authors' Comment: Celebrities often surround themselves with people paid for their expertise in various fields, such as Mr. Allen mentioned. Often, these specialists are the ones who have to be sold first.

❧ Creative Odds and Ends ❧

This potpourri of creative techniques on how to get people to return your calls just don't fit any of the ten other categories. Frankly, some of these are so innovative, they are "uncategorizable"! So, if you haven't found your "ideal" approach yet, read on. Even if you have one and you've already successfully field-tested it, you may still have room for another that fits a special situation.

✑ Scare Tactics ✐

Liz Smith

Newsday–New York Post–Los Angeles Times writer. Liz states that, after writing a gossip column for 20 years, she has to put on her thinking cap to remember what it's like not to have a call returned!

I confess that a lot of famous people don't want to take my call, but just the same I generally hear back either from them or from an assistant or PR person. I suppose my calls constitute a kind of reign-of-terror blackmail or at least incipient blackmail, but that's not so. You might think that the only real reason they call me back is in hope of damage control, but that's not so either.

If I were an unknown person—and I certainly was for many years—I think I'd try to get a return call by leaving the message, "This is important, so please tell Mr. Jones it would be in his best interest to call me." This is the same kind of message I leave when an important person doesn't call me back the first time around. It generally gets a response.

Actually, I suppose one might say there is nothing quite like scaring people to death. In fact, I'm so afraid of scaring people, I often say, "This is Liz Smith calling and it's not important." Nowadays, this also gets my calls returned.

I can't resist telling you about the favorite phone call I've had returned, when I was writing an article for *Cosmopolitan* on what famous people like as their favorite desserts. As a young, unknown freelance writer, I had left a message for Joan Crawford to return my call.

When my phone rang at 7:00 A.M., I was in a sound sleep. I figured only one person would call me that early in the morning. I shouted into the phone, "What the hell do you mean calling me this time of morning, you idiot!" Of course, I was mistaken. It was not my friend but Joan Crawford on the line.

A frigid Ms. Crawford answered, "Well, excuse me. This is Joan Crawford," and she hung up.

I quickly called to apologize. Ms. Crawford accepted my apology and said, "And now, Miss Smith—if you are awake—my favorite dessert is a great, big, juicy dill pickle!"

Authors' Comment: Liz Smith reminds us of the power of the press. But the reason Joan Crawford returned her call even after being shouted at is something that's very basic: *Liz had something she wanted!* Ms. Crawford wanted to be in her column.

❧ Say It with Fire ☙ (If Flowers Don't Work)

Cindy Adams

A New York Post columnist, Cindy says that, after a dozen attempts to get through to a prospect, a friend of hers refused to be discouraged.

Instead of losing her cool, she sent the man a dozen roses with a note that read, "I've called you a dozen times, and you never return my calls." Now how could a man not return a call after he's received flowers? He called her immediately.

Another friend of mine was in the same boat and unable to convince a receptionist to put her calls through. It wasn't her nature to send flowers. So this friend marched into the guy's reception area, and whipped a handwritten note out of her purse.

Then she lit a match and singed its four corners, leaving only her name and number in the middle of the paper. "Give this to him," she ordered and stormed out the door.

My friend got a call from the guy later that same afternoon.

Personally, I prefer flowers.

Authors' Comment: You're playing with fire when you use this approach to get your foot in the door.

❦ I'll Be in Denver on Wednesday ❧

Bill Rasmussen

In 1979, Bill cofounded ESPN with his son Scott. While ESPN is a household word today—all over the world—when the Rasmussens first started out, there were many doubting Thomases.

In the early days, nobody thought about 24-hour-a-day television. Even HBO was on only five hours a night, and overnight network television such as CNN or WTBS was still to come. So we weren't surprised that people thought we were crazy to plan a 24-hour single-interest channel for sports. Not only that, we planned to sell advertising on cable television—something that had never been done—24 hours a day!

To get the greatest number of subscribers, we had to sell to the biggest multiple system operators (MSOs) such as Teleprompter, TCI-Communications, and United Cable. The top ten MSOs in the country had a combined total of 13 million cable subscribers (there are 70 million in the United States today). I had a list of the names and phone numbers of the top dogs—the CEO, the president, or whoever the decision maker was—and I started making my calls.

Knowing full well that hardly anyone knew about our tiny, new company, I decided to act as if everyone had already heard of ESPN.

For instance, my secretary made a call to Gene Schneider, president of United Cable in Denver, one of the early pioneers in the cable industry. She said to Schneider's secretary:

> Hello, I'm calling for Bill Rasmussen, CEO of ESPN. Mr. Rasmussen will be in Denver on Wednesday, and I'm calling to schedule an appointment for him with Mr. Schneider. Mr. Rasmussen wants to fill him in on an exciting opportunity in cable television.

As soon as she booked an appointment with Schneider, I bought an airline ticket. Once I was safely booked to see Schneider at United Cable, I called John Malone at TCI and said, "I'll be in Denver on Wednesday to meet with Gene Schneider of United Cable about an exciting opportunity in cable television. While I'm in town, I'd like to meet with you." I did the same with Bill Daniels at Daniels Associates, also a major player in cable television located in Denver. Then I called Jim Whitson, president of Sammons Communications and said I'd swing by Dallas to meet with him on my way back home.

Amazingly, I was able to meet with the big guns at eight of the top ten cable television companies. It was a piece of cake!

❧ The Little Touches *Do* ❧
Make a Difference

Barry J. Farber

President of Farber Training Systems Inc. in Florham Park, New Jersey, and author of several best-selling books, including Diamond in the Rough. *He claims the success secret of highly successful businesspeople is building relationships. The following illustrates how Barry accomplishes this during his initial calls to prospects.*

I ask a lot of questions to find out what people like to do. I want to know their hobbies and how they spend their recreational time. For instance, when a secretary told me her boss was very busy because he was getting ready to go on his vacation, I casually asked, "Where's he going?"

"He's taking his family on a long overdue trip to the Smokies," she replied.

During my lunch hour, I stopped at the local American Automobile Club and picked up every piece of literature they had on the Smokies. Then I overnighted it to the man.

When he returned from his vacation, he called to thank me for being so considerate. He also placed an order for 500 copies of my book and has been reordering ever since.

The Girl, the White Rose, and the Parking Space

Terri Sjodin

A full-time professional trainer whose offices are based in Fountain Valley, California. Terri is the author of Sales Speak, Everybody Sells Something. *She tells the following story about her first commissioned sales position after graduating from college.*

I worked for a company that promoted training seminars for sales organizations. For one program, my job was to sign up real estate agencies and convince them to buy tickets for their salespeople. The ABC Real Estate Firm had 12 offices, each with 50 to 100 agents, but no matter how many times I called the president, the gatekeeper always said, "Send him some literature," or "We're a closed office and don't use outside vendors."

I was about to give up but, luckily for me, I saw the movie *Wall Street*. I marveled at how the young stockbroker was able to get into Gecko's office. First he sent Gecko a box of his favorite cigars as a birthday present, then waited six hours in his waiting room. Finally, he got in to see the Wall Street power broker and made the deal.

If it could happen in the movies, why not in real life? I thought. That's when I came up with a novel approach to see ABC's president.

On Monday, I called his office and asked his secretary what time he normally came to the office in the morning. "Between seven to nine," I was told.

The next morning at seven, I stood in his parking space holding a white rose, which symbolizes friendship and integrity. I figured this way nobody could hang up on me: The worst thing that could happen was that he'd run me over!

Of course, as he approached the parking space, I stepped aside and let him park his car. Then I approached him as he opened his door.

"Are you Mr. Smith?" I asked, handing him the flower.

"Yes. Who are you?"

"I'm Terri Sjodin. May I have ten minutes of your time?"

"I'll give you two minutes from this door to my office door," he said.

I could tell he got a kick out of me because I was trying so hard. We set up an appointment for me to see him the following morning. The next day we talked for about an hour, and he allowed me to present my programs to his entire sales staff. That month I became our company's top salesperson, and I have never forgotten the message of the white rose: A little tenacity, a little creativity, a little courage, and a little kindness go a long way.

> ***Authors' Comment:*** Flowers work well when used with women. As we see it, a man could have equal success if his prospect was a woman!

❧ Staying in Control ❧

Richard Schultz

Founder and CEO of National Revenue Corporation, one of the largest collection agencies in the United States. His firm's annual collection placements exceed $2 billion.

Too many salespeople lose control by volunteering too much information in their attempt to get past gatekeepers. Never tell more than they ask. Give the briefest possible answer, and then *ask a question.* That's the key: Always come back with a question so that they have to think about their answer, not a question to come back at you with.

It goes like this:

"I'd like to speak to Mr. Williams, please."

"May I tell him who's calling?"

"Richard Schultz. Is he in, please?"

"Yes, he is. What company are you with, Mr. Schultz?"

At this point I speak very slowly. "National Revenue. Would you tell him I'm on the phone, please?"

Notice that I've asked three times for the secretary to connect me with him. Persistence pays off in this game of verbal volleyball. No matter how many times you ask, gatekeepers come back with two or three screening questions. They feel as though that's their job. Therefore, when they ask who's calling, I don't say, "Richard Schultz of National Revenue." I make them ask me for the information. And I always answer their question with a question.

If they're very persistent and ask the nature of my business, as a last resort I'll reply, "It's a confidential financial matter. Would you please tell Mr. Williams that I would like to speak to him? If he's too busy, I'll be happy to call back."

Authors' Comment: You have to practice this one to get it down pat. Once you master it, we believe it's great material. But be cautious. It's not the kind of approach that promises to win friends!

How's This for Fast Service?

Tom Hopkins

President of Tom Hopkins International, based in Scottsdale, Arizona. Tom is considered one of the nation's leading sales trainers. He has authored seven books, including How to Master the Art of Selling.

Early in my career, I sold real estate. During this time, I learned an important lesson about the telephone: When used correctly, it is a masterful tool for making appointments. Whenever anyone called me about a property, I had one objective in mind: to convert the call into an in-person meeting.

One day a man called me in response to the listing of a home I had placed in a newspaper ad. In an abrupt manner, he identified the listing and said, "Just give me the address of the home, and I'll drive by to take a look at it."

I remembered my mission. "I'm Tom Hopkins," I said, "and to whom am I speaking?"

"That's not important. I just want the address of the house advertised in the paper," he answered.

"I'll be happy to show it to. . . ."

"Perhaps you didn't hear what I said," he interrupted. "I can look at it by myself. *You're what I don't want!* I don't want to be bothered by a real estate agent."

"Sir," I said politely, "one of the conditions in the contract with the homeowner is that an agent accompanies each prospect to the property. I'm available now, or would 3:00 be more convenient?" I had given him an alternate of choice, just as I was taught in a training class!

"Don't give me that crap," he said, raising his voice. "I don't want to meet with a real estate agent. I can't stand you people. Now if you'll just give me the address. . . ."

"Why don't we do this?" I butted in. "I know a way we can accomplish what you want. I'll just call the seller and ask for his permission. If he says yes, then I'll get right back to you with the address. What's your number? I can call you right back."

"You can't call me back!" he shouted. "I'm in a phone booth."

"Can you see the street signs from where you are?" I asked.

"Yeah, I'm at the corner of Los Angeles and Patricia Avenue."

He was only a half block from my office, but I wasn't about to tell him that. Instead I said, "Hold on a second, will you, and let me get the details on the home."

As soon as I put him on hold, I grabbed the file, ran out to my car, and screeched on down to Los Angeles and Patricia.

When I knocked on the phone booth door, he motioned for me to go away. I continued to knock, and finally he opened the door. "Can't you see I'm on hold?"

"You can hang up, sir. I'm Tom Hopkins."

"You're—you're . . . ," he stammered weakly. "I don't believe you. . . ."

"Yeah, I just had to meet you in person," I said. "I know I can give you better service than any real estate agent in town and that's why I popped over."

With that, a wide grin appeared on his face, and he warmly shook my hand.

Not only did I sell a lovely home to this man and his wife, but, over a period of time, they bought two other properties from me.

Authors' Comment: This story offers several tips. First, note that Tom Hopkins stayed in control, which is essential with this kind of prospect. Second, it demonstrates that thinking on your feet is essential. Third, it proves that the "tough ones" can be converted into sales. So don't give up when you first meet resistance.

❧ After Hours ❧

Kathleen Beckett

Kathleen, who lives in New York City, she is a freelance writer for Harpers Bazaar, Glamour, Vogue, Elle, Allure, The New York Post, *and* The New York Times.

The easiest way I know to get through to a VIP is to call after 5:30 when the secretary has left for the day. The VIP then picks up the phone. You can also reverse this and call early in the morning before the secretary gets to work. I have always found that successful people became successful because they work long hours!

Authors' Comment: If the gatekeeper gives you a difficult time, call Ms. Big after hours when she answers her own phone.

❧ Lunch Is on Me ❧

Naura Hayden

Naura also told us about the following method that she uses to get an appointment with a VIP.

Several years ago, I joined the Friar's Club in New York. Ever since, I've been using it as a tool to make lunch appointments with people. I simply leave a message on an answering machine or tell the secretary, "This is Naura Hayden, and I'd like to take you (him/her) to lunch at the Friar's Club. Please call me back at 999-9999 so that we can arrange a date."

I always get a return call and lunch date. The only time it doesn't work is when I call people who are already members of the Friar's Club. They don't need me to eat there! I suppose it's the thrill of never knowing who will be sitting at the next table that makes people want to have lunch with me at the Friar's Club!

Authors' Comment: There is only one Friar's Club and it's in New York City. However, if it makes sense economically, you can invite your VIP to an exclusive country club or city club where you are a member, or perhaps to an exclusive restaurant in your area. The key thing is to choose a very special place.

❦ The Seminar ❧

David Finkel

*President and chief executive officer of Signature Home Care, Inc., one of the
premier home care companies in the United States. His company is
headquartered in Irving, Texas.*

Back in the mid-1980s, as CEO of a hospital in Columbia, Missouri, I spent a significant portion of my time soliciting physicians to utilize our 350-bed facility. Of course, we had plenty of competition, including several other private hospitals and some operated by the university and the county. Since the doctors in the area had many alternatives and they generally knew in advance my reason for calling them, they simply avoided taking my call.

It happened that a friend who was a neurologist had invited me to a dinner party. After we ate, he gave me a tour of his home—and his woodworking shop in his garage. Woodworking was his hobby, and to my surprise I discovered that many physicians also shared the same pastime. I then realized that this could be the answer to my problem. After researching the woodworking field, I invited Ian Kirby, a world-renowned British woodworking expert, to Columbia to conduct a series of seminars, limited to 20 persons per session. Altogether, 600 doctors received an invitation with instructions to call my secretary for reservations. Well, we were so besieged with calls, we couldn't accommodate everybody. So with the prime prospects we wanted to use our hospital beds, I instructed my secretary to say, "I'm sorry, but the seminar is full and we can't take any more registrants. However, if you call David Finkel, I am certain he'll be able to find some way to accommodate you."

Then, when they called, I said, "I'd like to give you a tour of our hospital, and while you're here, I'll personally give you your seminar tickets." Once I had them on my own turf, promoting the merits of my hospital was easy.

Authors' Comment: Dave Finkel figured out a way to get otherwise disinterested prospects to attend his seminar. What did he do? He figured out what it was that really turned them on. If he could get a large group of busy doctors to come to a series of woodworking seminars, then just think what you can do, with some imagination, in your field.

❧ Now Hear This . . . ❧

Peter Connolly

Senior vice-president of worldwide communication for The Polo Ralph Lauren Corporation in New York City. He was previously vice-president of marketing at Ikea, an international chain of furniture stores.

In 1990, we had just one month to go before the opening in Elizabeth, New Jersey of what was to be Ikea's flagship store in all of North America. As the store's general manager, I was being bombarded with calls from people wanting us to take out ads in all sorts of newspapers and magazines, as well as wanting us to buy time on radio and television. With the opening of our huge store, as much as I wanted to, there simply wasn't enough time to return most of the calls that kept pouring in.

One caller, a John Quinn who didn't get called back, decided to do something unusual to get my attention. Let me explain that, being new in Elizabeth, I didn't know who John Quinn was. He was one of the area's most prominent businesspeople and owner and president of WJDM Radio—1530 on the AM dial—the most popular station in Elizabeth. He was president of the Chamber of Commerce and had a lot of political clout throughout the state, starting with the governor. John Quinn was also a determined man who didn't like to be told no!

While driving to the store one morning, I tuned into WJDM and to my surprise heard an announcer say that the City of Elizabeth was excited to become the home of the new Ikea store. Of course, I became excited too, especially when he said, "We also want to welcome Peter Connolly, the new general manager. And Pete, give us a call, because we'd like to work with you in assuring Ikea's success in Elizabeth."

After being addressed directly on the air, I figured I had to call John Quinn right away. After our conversation, Ikea began advertising on WJDM, and John Quinn and I have been good friends ever since.

Authors' Comment: Once again, we see that innovation does the job. Understandably, we realize that John Quinn had a radio station at his disposal to get Peter Connolly's attention—and you don't! Nonetheless, this should get your creative juices flowing.

❧ Let's Do Lunch ❧

Linda McKarney

*Based in Sacramento, California, Linda is an account representative with
Arcus Data Security, one of the nation's leading companies in the
field of disaster recovery and off-site data storage.*

I had a serious problem. After one of my larger accounts, Kaiser Foundation
Health Plan, Inc., hired Don Edwards as its new director of data processing, I
wasn't able to set up an appointment with him. Since Edwards was his company's
number-one decision maker, a meeting was critical. No matter how much time I
spent talking to his subordinates, unless he gave the go-ahead, a major part of the
business I could do with his company would be farmed out to other vendors.

"If I could only get through to him," I kept telling myself. I knew his company would benefit from what we had to offer.

However, Edwards wouldn't take my personal calls. His secretary repeatedly told me, "He's booked solid for the next two months."

"Do you think I could I see him for just five minutes?" I pleaded.

"I'm sorry, but there's nothing I can do," she replied. "It's out of my hands."

I knew I had to think of something. "He has to eat," I said. "What about during lunch?"

"Well, Mr. Edwards takes exactly one hour for lunch," she confided. "He leaves
the office right at noon and returns promptly for a one o'clock meeting every day."

Knowing there wasn't a decent place to eat in the vicinity, I figured it would
take a minimum of 20 minutes driving time each way to and from a restaurant.
That would leave us only 20 minutes to gulp down our food. Obviously that
wouldn't work.

A few days later I had a brainstorm. I called the secretary. "Tell Mr.
Edwards to put me down for lunch at noon on Friday," I said enthusiastically. "I

will pick him up and take him to one of the best lunch spots he's ever been to—and it's only five minutes from the office."

"Where is it?" she asked excitedly.

"It's a secret, but I promise you he's going to love it! It's guaranteed to be a lunch he'll never forget!"

She delivered my message and evidently it intrigued Edwards. He agreed to go.

The first thing he asked upon getting into my car was, "Where are you taking me?"

"You'll find out in just five minutes," I answered.

I drove to a lovely park, parked my car, and announced, "We're here."

"Here?" he questioned.

I pointed to a picnic table in a shaded area with a beautiful view. I opened my trunk, revealing the picnic basket I had prepared, and Edwards carried it over to the bench. I spread a red-and-white checked tablecloth over the tabletop, and took out two place settings complete with wine glasses, which I filled with gourmet herbal iced tea. Then I served a sumptuous meal consisting of deli food.

California weather is generally ideal for picnics, but we were blessed with a particularly gorgeous day.

"I must admit this is a beautiful setting for a meal," he said approvingly.

As he ate, I was able to tell him everything I wanted him to know about our services and products.

Now that Don is settled into his new position, I'm able to see him more frequently. Perhaps the reason is that Kaiser has recently become my biggest account!

Don constantly reminds me of our picnic, and tells everyone it was the best vendor lunch he's ever had!

Authors' Comment: If you don't have a scenic park site nearby to have a picnic, try taking a catered lunch to Ms. Big's office!

Whadda Ya Mean He Doesn't Work Here Anymore?

Sherri Gilman

*Vice-president of Jericho Promotions, Sherri provides the following technique she
has used to land appointments with difficult-to-see VIPs. Sherri claims she
landed her biggest account with this technique.*

To use this approach, you have to do your homework. First, you have to know in advance that a particular executive—say, Bob Brown—has recently left XYZ Company. Second, timing is vital. Your call must be made within a two- to three-week window *after* Brown's replacement has been hired. It works like this:

"I'm calling for Bob Brown," I say matter-of-factly to the new executive's secretary.

"I'm sorry but Mr. Brown is no longer with XYZ Company," she replies.

Then, with a slight panic in my voice, I say, "Whadda ya mean, he doesn't work here anymore?" Before she can reply, I explain in a rambling way that Brown had asked me to prepare a presentation, which required an enormous amount of time and expense to get ready. "I'm ready to give my presentation, and I'm calling to schedule a time to get together."

Rather than asking to talk to Brown's replacement, I let the secretary suggest, "Let me put you through to Stan Smith, our new vice-president, who has Mr. Brown's old job."

Of course, this is exactly what I wanted in the first place: an opportunity to make a presentation to Mr. Smith!

As I said, this works when you have done your homework and know that a new executive has recently come aboard. Timing is crucial, because two to three weeks is not enough time for Mr. Jones to be settled in his new position. Yet it is soon enough that an important appointment could have been made with a predecessor, one that he naturally feels obligated to honor.

> **Authors' Comment:** A little chutzpa goes a long way, doesn't it? This one has a touch of urgency, which is what makes it work.

Not Just Another Pretty Pair of Legs

Anonymous

The vice-president of marketing at a large computer company,
who wishes to remain anonymous, told us the following story.

I arrived at my nine o'clock appointment a few minutes early for a meeting with Ralph Hill, vice-president of data processing for one of my biggest accounts, a big bank in Chicago.

Seated in an open office reception area, I waited patiently as I watched secretaries and office clerks labor at their work stations. To keep myself occupied, I eagerly reviewed my notes. I felt confident the bank would go for the $80,000 computer accessories package I was offering. After all, I had already established a long relationship with the bank.

Suddenly, my self-confidence was threatened. At exactly two minutes before the hour, who walks in? None other than Marilyn Conners, a sales rep with the only other company that was competing for the same piece of business. Oh no, I thought to myself, what poor timing!

While I knew my company had the best price and delivery, Marilyn was indeed an awesome competitor. She was bright and articulate. Beyond that, she had one special advantage with which I couldn't compete: She was absolutely, drop-dead beautiful! A tall blond with a gorgeous figure, she was dressed to kill. She wore a long dress with a sexy slit that went up well beyond the knee.

Marilyn's eyes met mine, but she ignored me and walked right past the secretary to Hill's open desk area. Towering over him, she said in a sexy voice, "Hi there, Ralphie. Do you have just a minute to see me?"

Without waiting for a reply, she seated herself on the chair next to his desk, and crossed her legs to allow the slit in her dress to reveal her long shapely leg. I could see she really got Hill's attention, and caused a major distraction for several of his co-workers. The room grew pretty quiet.

After 20 minutes of cooing and selling, she announced, "Of course, Ralphie dear, I'll personally handle your order. Now don't you forget, darling, when you need any supplies, you think of Marilyn." With that, she took out a sticker containing her name and phone number and stuck it on his phone. "Remember now, you just call Marilyn," she said in a loud, lusty whisper. On her way past me, she gave me one of those looks that says, "Hill is all mine, and I own him!"

Apparently too weak to get up from his desk, Hill said in a rather faint voice, "Jim, er, I'm ready to see you now."

I knew I had to think quickly; otherwise, I'd be no match for Marilyn.

As I stood to get out of my chair, with some effort I rolled up my pants legs to slightly above my knees. My voice was a bit gruffer than Marilyn's when I called out, "Thank you, Ralphie, sweetheart, for giving me this opportunity to see you."

At this point, everyone glanced away from their computer screens to watch me traipse over to Hill's desk. Sitting in the same chair that Marilyn had occupied, I crossed my legs to reveal the hairy legs above the argyle socks my wife had given me for Christmas. "You know, Ralph," I said in a serious tone, "these may be the ugliest legs you've ever seen, but I do have the price and the best delivery." His face turned slightly red. I said, "Here's the purchase order. I think we've earned the business. Now go ahead and put your okay on it."

When I said that, several men and women came out of their work stations to applaud. With their support, I knew I had the sale. "And when you need supplies, feel free to call Jim," I continued. With that, I took out my business card and scotch taped it over Marilyn's label. "I'm as near as your phone, Ralph."

I walked away from his desk toward the elevator, my cuffs still rolled up. The applause and laughter grew louder and louder as I marched past several work stations and made my grand exit.

Authors' Comment: This story clearly demonstrates what a touch of imagination can do when you're in a hole. It also proves that showmanship can be good salesmanship. As this marketing vice-president proves, it's okay to ham it up every now and then.

❧ Runaway Wife ❧

Robin Leach

Best known as the producer and host of ABC-TV's Lifestyles of the Rich and Famous. *He has produced a number of other TV series, as well as many TV specials.*

One of the greatest coups during my journalism career happened back in 1977 when Margaret Trudeaux made headlines as the "runaway wife" of Canada's prime minister. Her disappearance was the hottest news story of the day, and newspaper people all over the world were trying to get an interview with her. There must have been 800 reporters camped outside the New York apartment building where Mrs. Trudeaux was staying as the guest as Princess Yasmin Aga Khan, the daughter of actress Rita Hayworth and playboy Prince Aly Khan of Saudi Arabia. Every media person would have given a right arm for an exclusive interview, and I was no exception.

Since there was no way to phone, I handed a note to the doorman and asked him to pass it on to Mrs. Trudeaux. I wrote that, if she wanted to get back to Canada without having to fight her way through the horde of press at her doorstep, she should call my office. My note included a few tidbits on how I would accomplish what appeared to be a formidable task.

She called me immediately, and invited me to meet her in the Princess's apartment, where I made arrangements with her to carry out my pledge. I also got the exclusive interview I was after, something no other reporter in the world was able to secure.

The technique I used is something I have practiced throughout my career. When I want an "impossible-to-see" person to return my call, I figure out a way to offer something that fulfills a need. Of course, it takes some thinking and creativity to come up with the right thing. Then—and most importantly—you have to deliver, because in this kind of situation, you get only one shot!

Authors' Comment: You don't have to be a television celebrity like Robin Leach to figure out a way to offer something that fulfills your prospect's need. This is what good selling is all about!

❧ The Golf Challenge ❧

Michael Ebert

An account executive with BI™ Performance Services™. BI combines communications, training, measurement, and rewards/reinforcement into performance improvement programs for its Fortune 500 customers. While the company is headquartered in Minneapolis, Ebert is based in Troy, Michigan.

I was having a cup of coffee and reading *Crane's Business News* one morning when I ran across a story featuring the CEO of a large company. Now it happened that I had called this fellow several times over the past year but was unable to get through to him. The article presented him as a serious golf fan who was playing in a local pro-am tournament.

Upon discovering he was a golf enthusiast, I sent him a golf tournament invitation announcing "The BI Golf Challenge." This tournament would take place at a swank private country club in the area, which boasted a beautiful championship course. My announcement included this challenge:

> You and your best guy versus Michael Ebert and my best guy. If I win, I get a half hour of your time. If I lose, you don't have to talk to me.

A few days later, he called to accept the challenge and we set up a golf date. To make a long story short, they beat us, and I swear it had nothing to do with "customer golf." However, he still gave me the half hour, and his company is now one of our accounts.

Authors' Comment: Again, we are privy to a creative approach that appeals to a prospect's special interests. This technique happened to be a "golf tournament." It could have been anything from a fishing contest to a bridge game!

Making an Appointment with a Billionaire

Robert Shook

Coauthor Robert Shook tells a story that happened in 1980, when he was writing The Real Estate People *and called Harry Helmsley, New York City's multibillionaire real estate mogul.*

When I explained to his secretary that I wanted to set up a three-hour interview with him, she told me, "You'll have to speak to him personally about that."

"Then, please put me through to him," I replied.

"If you call Mr. Helmsley on Friday morning at 10:08, I will put you down for a five-minute telephone conversation with him."

At exactly 10:07, I placed the call. I was disappointed to be told, "I'm sorry, but an emergency came up and Mr. Helmsley is out of the office for the day." Another five-minute telephone appointment was set up for the following Thursday at 2:44 P.M.

Once again, I was told, "Mr. Helmsley is tied up but you can call him on Monday at 11:47 A.M."

Finally, on my third call, I was put through. Knowing I had only a few minutes to speak with him, I gave a quick explanation about the book I was writing and how much I wanted to write a chapter about him in it.

"Mr. Shook," he began, "give me one reason I should be in your book. What will it specifically do for me?"

"Mr. Helmsley, I can't think of how being in my book can personally benefit you," I answered. "But there is one very good reason you should consider an interview with me."

"What's that?" he asked.

"The real estate business has been very good to you, Mr. Helmsley."

"Yes," he interrupted, "It's been very, very good to me."

"As a way of paying your dues," I continued, "I believe you should share your philosophy and knowledge with others. Doing so will upgrade the real estate profession, and you will be performing a good deed for America."

There was a brief pause, and he said, "Would you kindly send me a letter giving me a brief explanation of your book? And then call me in a couple of weeks."

That afternoon, I sent an overnight package that included a two-page cover letter, my biosketch, three of my earlier books, and some newspaper and magazine articles about my writing career.

The next afternoon, my secretary came into my office and announced, "You have a phone call from Harry."

I picked up the receiver and heard, "Mr. Shook, this is Harry."

"Harry who?" I asked.

"This is Harry Helmsley. I have reviewed your material, and I'd be honored to be in your book, Mr. Shook."

"That's great, Harry," I blurted out. I thought to myself, "That's a good one. I'm calling him Harry, and he's calling me Mr. Shook."

"Let's set up a date for the interview," I said.

"You name the time, and I'll make sure I'm available," Helmsley told me.

"How's next Thursday morning at 10:37 sharp?" I asked.

Fortunately, Helmsley recognized the intended humor and laughed. "Let me write that down in my date book," he replied.

I should note three things about this story.

First, quite frankly. I'm not that quick and resourceful to have set up the appointment with the perfect ad-lib, "How's next Thursday morning at 10:37 sharp?" But after two previous conversations with his secretary, I had plenty of time to come up with that remark.

Second, when Helmsley asked why he should be in my book, I gave the only logical incentive for a man in his position to be interested in my project. Since he stood to benefit little, I realized the only way to win him over would be to appeal to his desire to be a Good Samaritan—and it worked.

Third, I followed up by quickly sending him an impressive package that would present me in the best possible light, along with a strong cover letter. I believe every businessperson should put together a package of this nature ready to present on the spur of the moment to a potential client.

Authors' Comment: To paraphrase F. Scott Fitzgerald, the super rich are no different from you or I; they just have more money. A good lesson to be learned is that the same things that work with other folk also work with the rich and powerful. After all, these people have a heart just like everyone else. People are people.

Section Twelve

❧ The Top Choices ☙

Everyone has a favorite technique. We believe this book works because it has something for everybody. While you probably already have a few of your own that you're anxious to field-test, if you haven't made up your mind, each of us has included our top five choices. What's more, we were able to convince our editor, Susan Barry, to share her choices with you.

Following these three lists, this final section concludes with 13 extra bonus tips. After you have finished reading this book, your telephone should be *ringing off the hook* with people returning your calls. If not, we recommend you read it again, and keep right on trying. Believe in this book! It works!

⤳ Shook's Top Five Choices ⤵

1. *Instant Results* by Eric Yaverbaum: When Eric told me about sending the box of "instant" products to the CEO at Club Med, his cleverness inspired me to collaborate with him on this book! You don't have to be a public relations person to use this technique. It will do the job for most of us!

2. *Your Boss Will Appreciate It* by Buck Rodgers: This is an excellent approach for an executive. When you deliver the message in a very businesslike manner (as Buck does it), most secretaries put the call through without hesitation.

3. *Great News* by Lisa Lapides: As Lisa says, everyone likes to hear great news. Consequently, this approach should be appropriate for all prospects, and you can customize it for any circumstance. For instance, after hearing Lisa, I tested it on a few people I wanted to interview for this book. When they came on the line to ask what the great news was, I enthusiastically said, "The great news is that I am going to put you in a Shook book!" I passed this one on to a real estate broker who also reported success with it. When his prospect asked about the great news, the broker said, "I have a new listing on a home that is perfect for you and your family." He made the appointment and later the sale!

4. *Birthday Greetings!* by Edward Lubin: As Eddie explains, since most people don't get many happy birthday calls, most secretaries assume that your call is personal and put you through with no questions. Likewise, you give a person a delightful surprise by starting the conversation with a birthday greeting. The recipient is likely to respond with, "How did you know it was my birthday?" Your explanation

demonstrates that you were resourceful—and thoughtful enough to do your homework before placing the call!

5. *Let's Do Lunch* by Linda McKarney: While this is a wonderful story, the idea must be tweaked to accommodate various situations. If there is a nearby picnic spot with a charming setting, great! If not, improvise! And be selective with whom you picnic! I told this story to a friend who lives in New York City, and she can't wait until the weather permits her to take a prospective client by limousine to Central Park! She's also planning a catered lunch from one of New York's famous restaurants, to be served in a client's board room!

❧ Yaverbaum's Top Five Choices ❧

1. *The Checkoff List* by Hal Becker: This simple fax works like a charm. When Hal submitted it to us, I field-tested it, sending it out word for word. Amazingly, people returned my calls like clockwork. I know that, if somebody faxed this list to me, I'd laugh—and it would remind me in a pleasant way to return the call.

2. *The Early Bird* by Bettye Hardeman: I have learned that people respond more favorably when I call them at home rather than at the office. After all, the workplace is generally a more hectic, stressful environment. So when people are called at their residence, they are usually more relaxed and friendly. I fully agree with Bettye that successful people are early risers, and consequently I have no problem putting a call through to them the first thing in the morning. It's also a time of the day when there's far less competition for their time!

3. *The Referral* by Jay Bernstein: Whenever I have a third party's name, I always mention it as a door opener. Using a VIP's name is an especially powerful way to get a call-back because people don't want to offend the VIP! What is she going to think if you refused to talk to somebody she referred to you? Think about it. If your boss or the governor told somebody to call you, would you refuse to talk to the caller? Not likely.

4. *A Lesson in Perseverance* by Rich Luisi: About halfway through the writing of the manuscript, our researcher called Rich. I was well aware of what she was going through with him as I followed her daily progress reports. Admittedly, at one point I thought it was time to give up on him, but she persisted. Consequently, he taught her—and us— a valuable lesson, which we are delighted to pass on to you.

5. *Whadda Ya Mean He Doesn't Work Here Anymore?* by Sherri Gilman: The ingenuity behind this approach is its timing. And when the question is said in a frantic way (which Sherri has mastered), the response is terrific. For the past nine years, I've observed Sherri's use of this technique, and it truly works! Sherri has made a believer out of me!

❧ The Editor's Top Five Choices ❧

Our editor, Susan Barry, has graciously listed her favorites.

1. *Just the Fax, Ma'am* by Margaret Torme: I like this because, in addition to being clever, it's right to the point. And it's so easy to implement. You can simply copy it right out of the book!

2. *Instant Results* by Eric Yaverbaum: It's hard to imagine anyone who wouldn't return a telephone call after receiving this "instant" package. I recommend trying it soon. You could get the jump on the other readers of this book who start sending their instant packages. This is too clever not to be copied.

3. *The Plant* by Lezlie Campeggi: Sending an expensive plant is appreciated by most people. So I think it will warrant a returned call. Naturally, there are many other gifts you can send that will be equally appreciated. But don't go overboard. Not only is it expensive, but there's such a thing as overkill. Some people consider an expensive gift as a form of payola.

4. *Using the Negative to Generate a Positive Response* by Elizabeth Graham: I told our public relations people this wonderful story. They loved it and vowed to field-test it. They did and it works. Remember, too, that many of us work in a large organization where we have "internal customers." This is an excellent technique to use for those calls.

5. *The Skeleton* by Terri Williams: I like Terri Williams' approach because it's funny and nonoffensive. In addition, it demonstrates that you don't have to send an expensive gift to get your calls returned.

❧ 13 Bonus Tips ❧

During the writing of our manuscript, along with the many excellent stories, hundreds of tidbits were submitted. While we could not use all of them, we have gleaned the following 13 bonus tips to share with our readers:

1. *Having a positive attitude is vital.* Through your voice, people can sense whether you have confidence in yourself, your company, and your product.

2. *Always be courteous to the gatekeeper.* As one VIP stated, "When asked about the nature of his call, a salesperson once said to my secretary, 'It's none of your business. He knows me!' Well, I didn't know him, and I do not care to do business with anyone who is rude to my employees!"

3. *Keep your answers brief.* There is no point in giving a long explanation to the gatekeeper. The secretary is not the decision maker. So your first approach should be brief and direct. "My name is Tom Jones with the American Corporation. May I please speak to Mr. Smith?" Identify yourself and ask to speak to the prospect. Frequently this is enough to put you through immediately.

4. *Understand the job of gatekeepers.* Their job is not to keep calls from being put through to the boss, but to screen calls. Certain ones are put through. It's essential to remember that every businessperson must communicate with the outside world. Refusal to do so would be a sure way to fail. With this in mind, the gatekeeper does not intend to eliminate all incoming calls. Your job is simply to make sure your own calls are treated with importance.

5. *Call early.* Make sure you're the first voicemail message of the day, even if it means calling at 6:00 A.M. People who receive lots of messages may not listen to all of them, or they may be interrupted after listening to only the first few!

6. *Start and end your voicemail message with your name and phone number.* Remember, you want to make it easy for people to call you back.

7. *Respect your prospect's schedule.* For example, a jewelry store owner is going to be busy during the Christmas shopping season, a restaurant owner during the lunch and dinner hours, etc. We suggest you apply some common sense before you place your call. It's wise to pick a slow time of the day when you're less apt to interrupt an otherwise busy person.

8. *Be persistent.* Calls go unreturned for many reasons. Don't give up on the first call that isn't returned.

9. *Be sure to talk to the decision maker.* Within an organization, many people who can say no actually do not have the authority to say yes. There is everything to lose and nothing to gain when you talk to a person in this capacity.

10. *Create a sense of urgency with the gatekeeper, but indirectly.* Rather than saying, "It's critical that Mr. Jones call me immediately," say something like, "Tell Mr. Jones that if he could call me today, I'd appreciate it." A message of this nature creates urgency but is not artificial.

11. *Recruit secretaries as your allies.* Find out their names on your first call, and, when you call back, use their names. "Jennifer, is there a time when Mr. Smith may be more available?" Most callers treat gatekeepers as nonpersons. By using their names and being polite, you win them over. Once you establish a rapport, ask them to do you a favor. Most people are receptive to helping other people. Say something like, "Jennifer, I would greatly appreciate it if you could tell me the best possible time to call Mr. Jones." Remember that Jennifer has the authority to put your call through to the boss. If she's in your corner, she will!

12. *Use a third party as an introduction.* When you mention the name of someone who is respected by the prospect, out of courtesy your call will be taken. Try to use the name of an important customer of your prospect. Nobody wants to risk offending someone who has been referred by a good customer!

13. *Nobody bats a thousand.* Don't allow yourself the luxury of being discouraged if a phone call is not returned. You're not alone in this area. If you were, there would be no need for this book!

About the Authors

Robert L. Shook is the best-selling author of more than 40 books, including *The Greatest Sales Stories Ever Told* (McGraw-Hill, 1995), *Hardball: How to Turn the Pressure On Without Turning Your Customer Off*, and *Successful Telephone Selling in the '90s*. Bob and his wife Elinor reside in Columbus, Ohio.

Eric Yaverbaum is the founder and president of one of New York's hottest PR firms. He is frequently on television and radio, including *CBS This Morning*, *The "Today" Show*, *CNN*, and *The Larry King Show*. Featured regularly in national media including *The New York Times*, *The Washington Post*, and *USA Today*, Eric is married, has a four-year-old daughter, and resides in New York City.